fairy houses

coloring book for adults

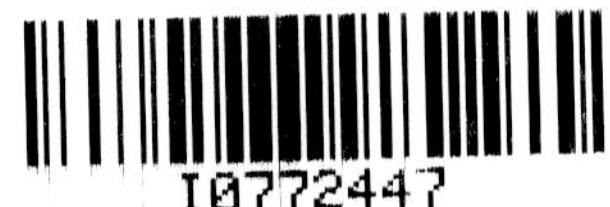

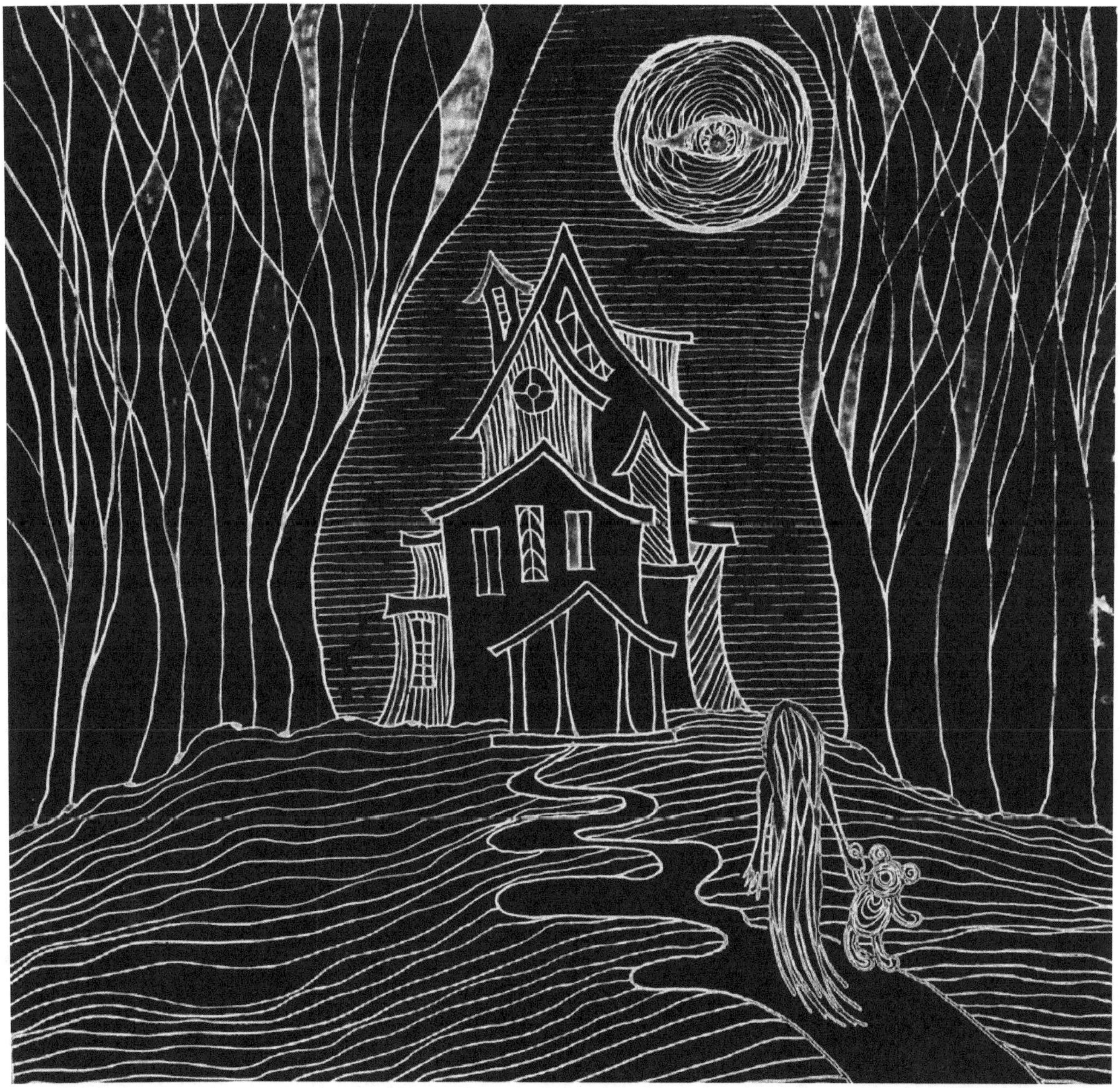

PAGE 1

test color

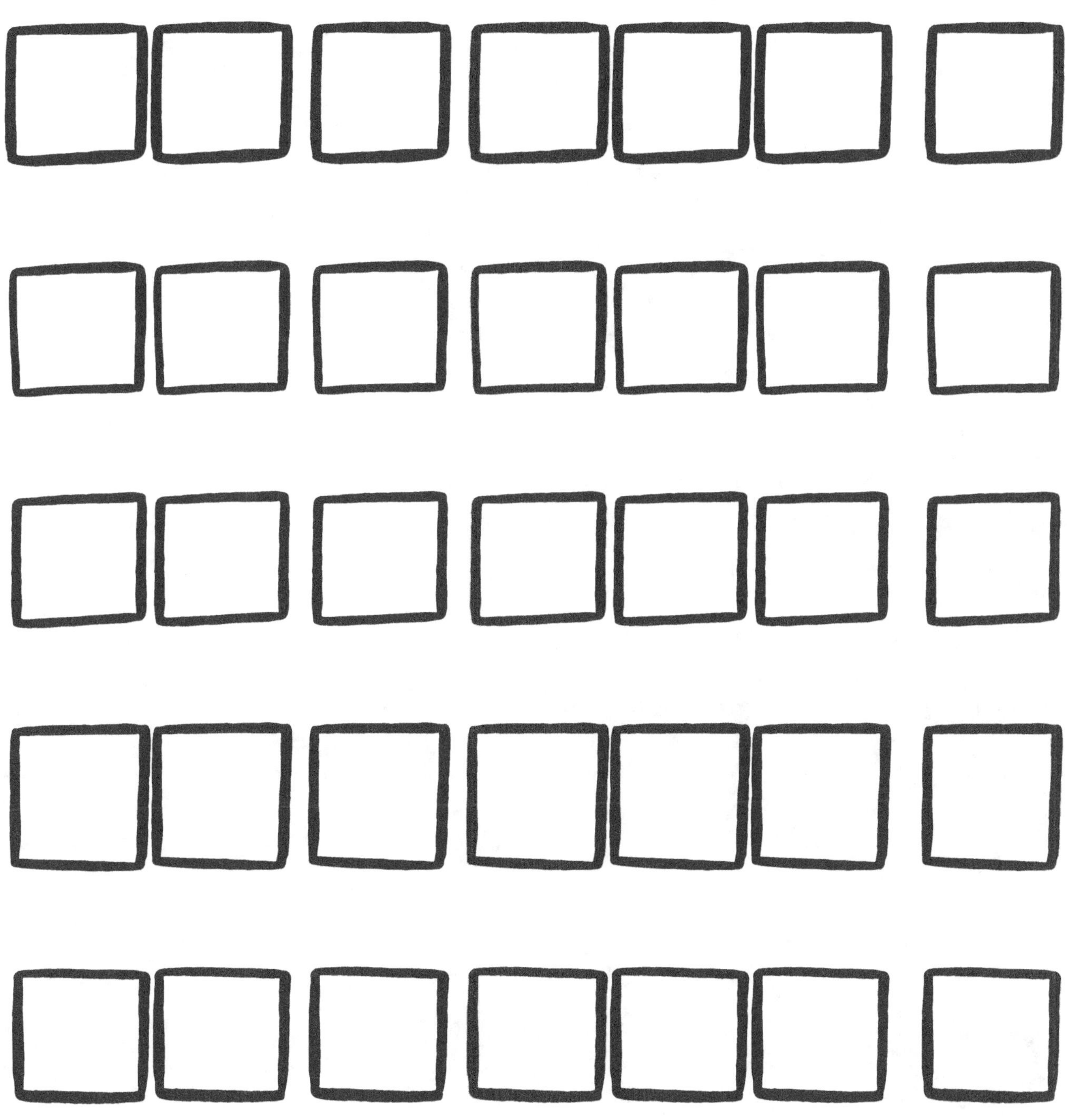

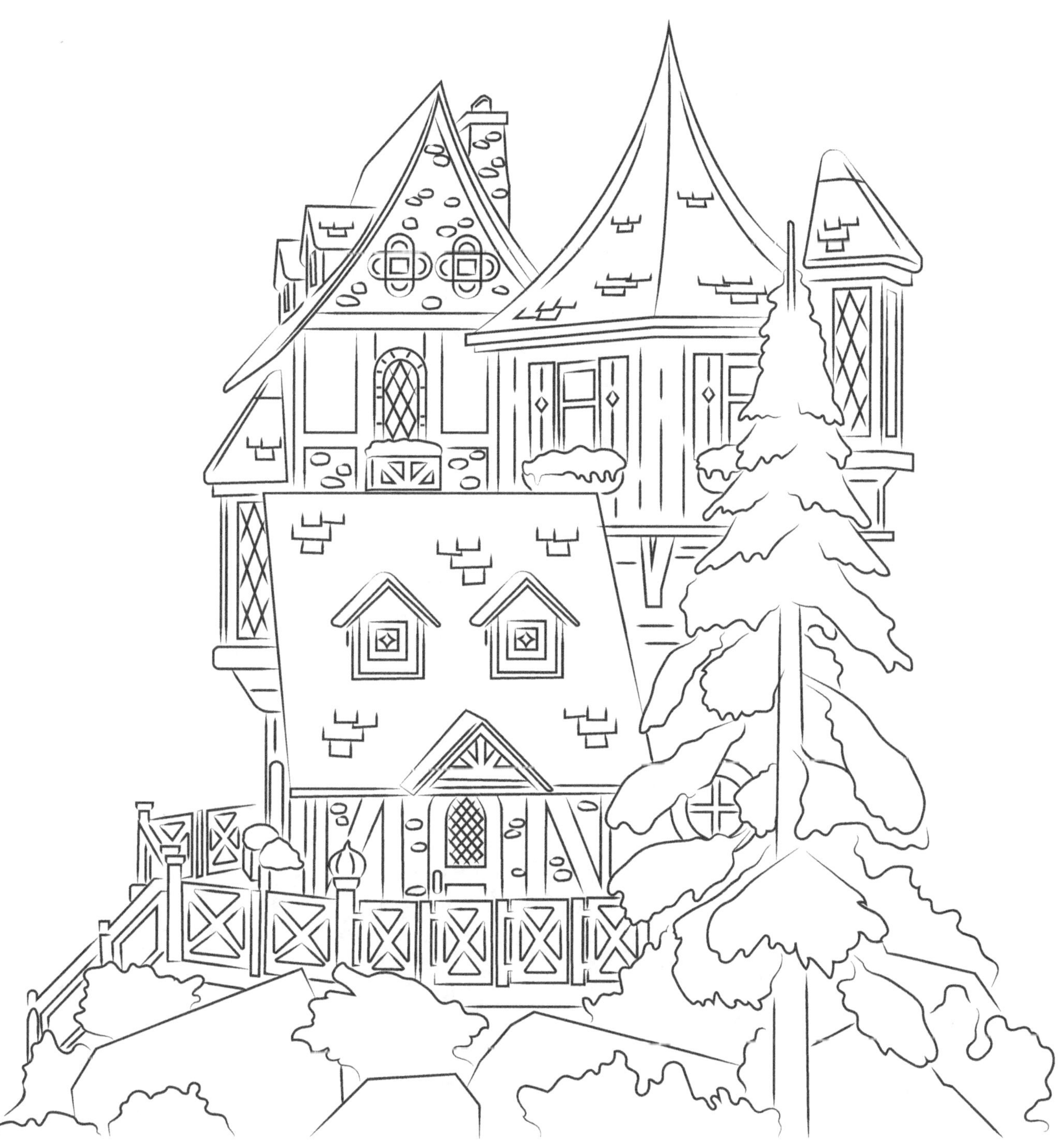

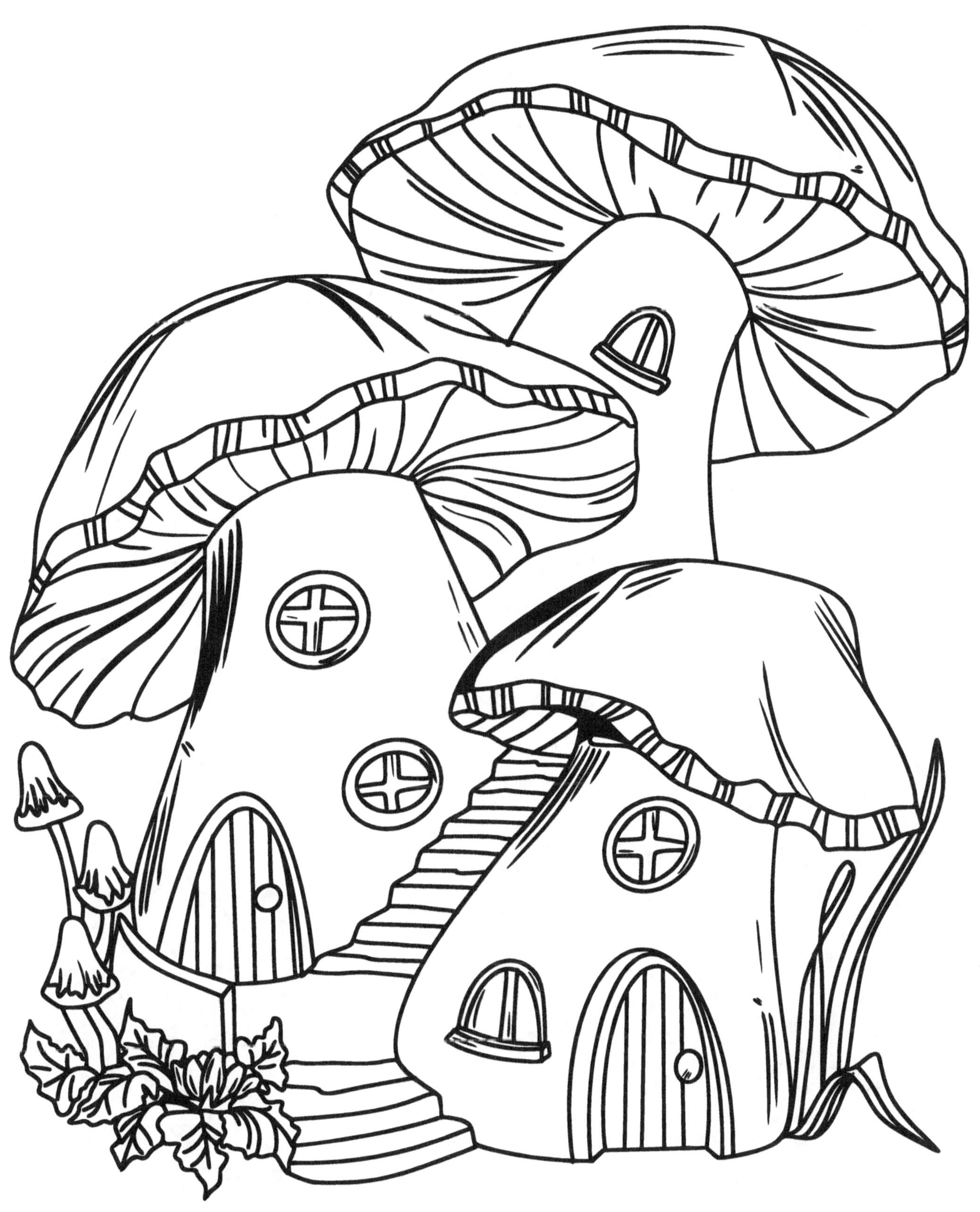

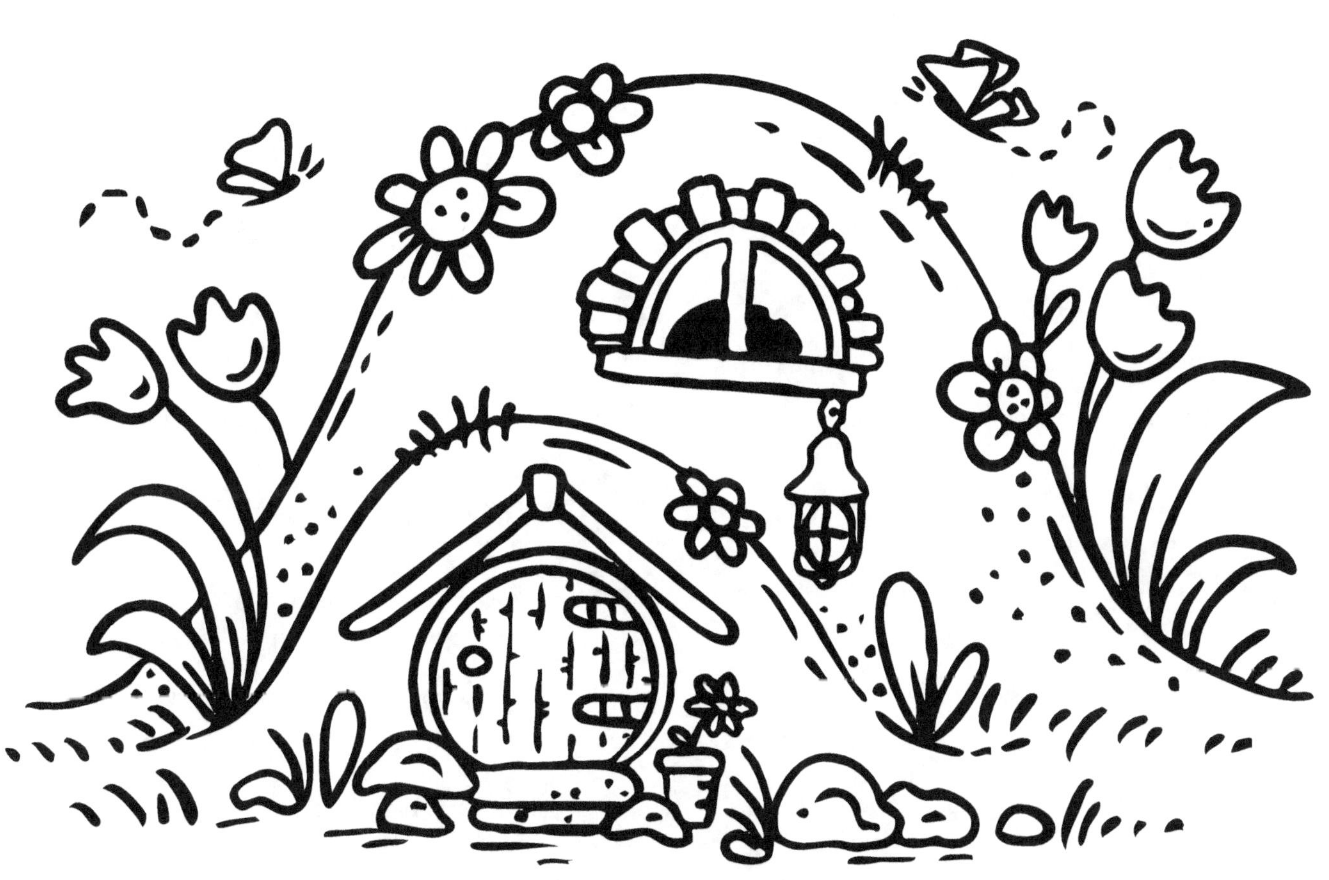

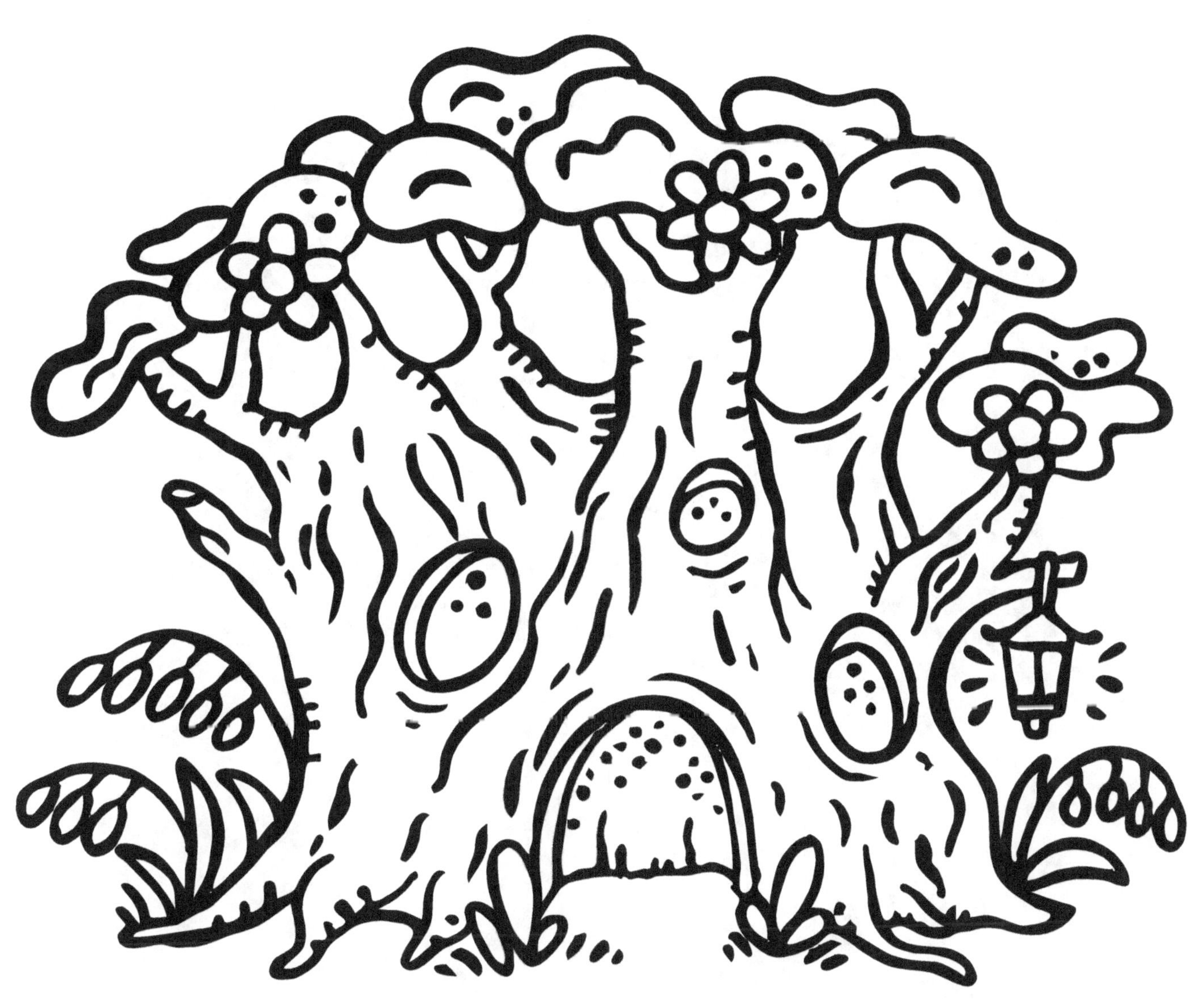

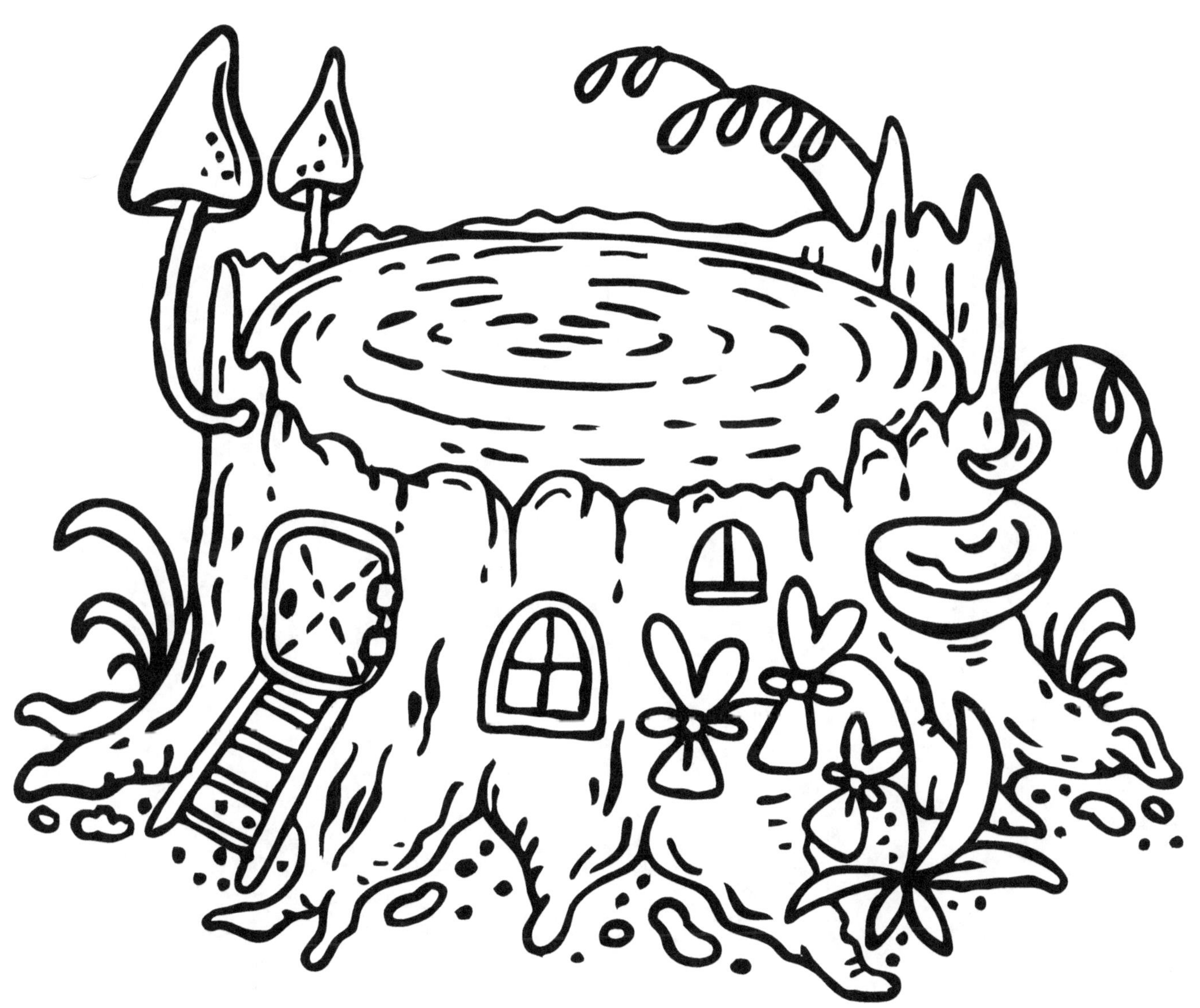

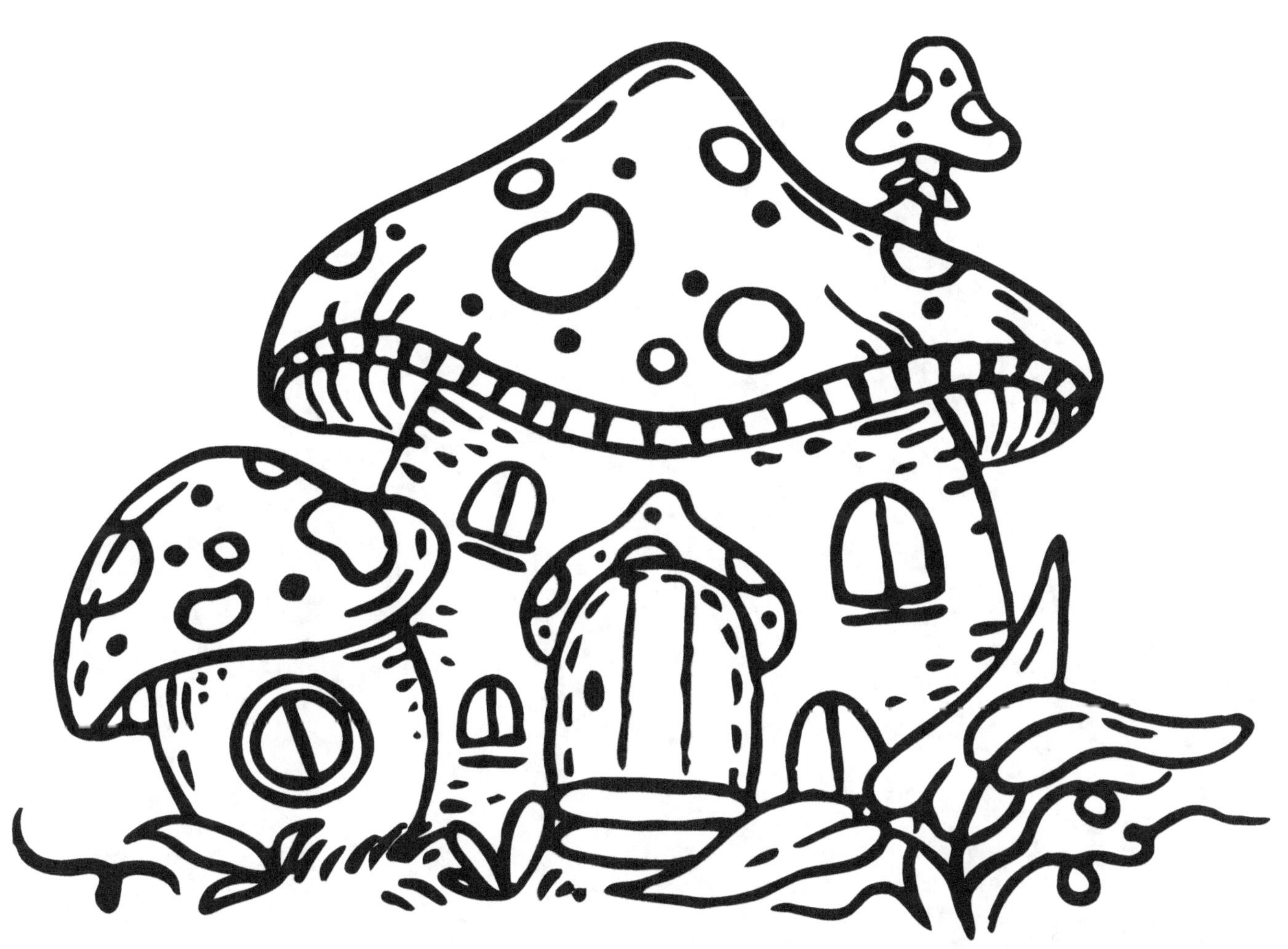

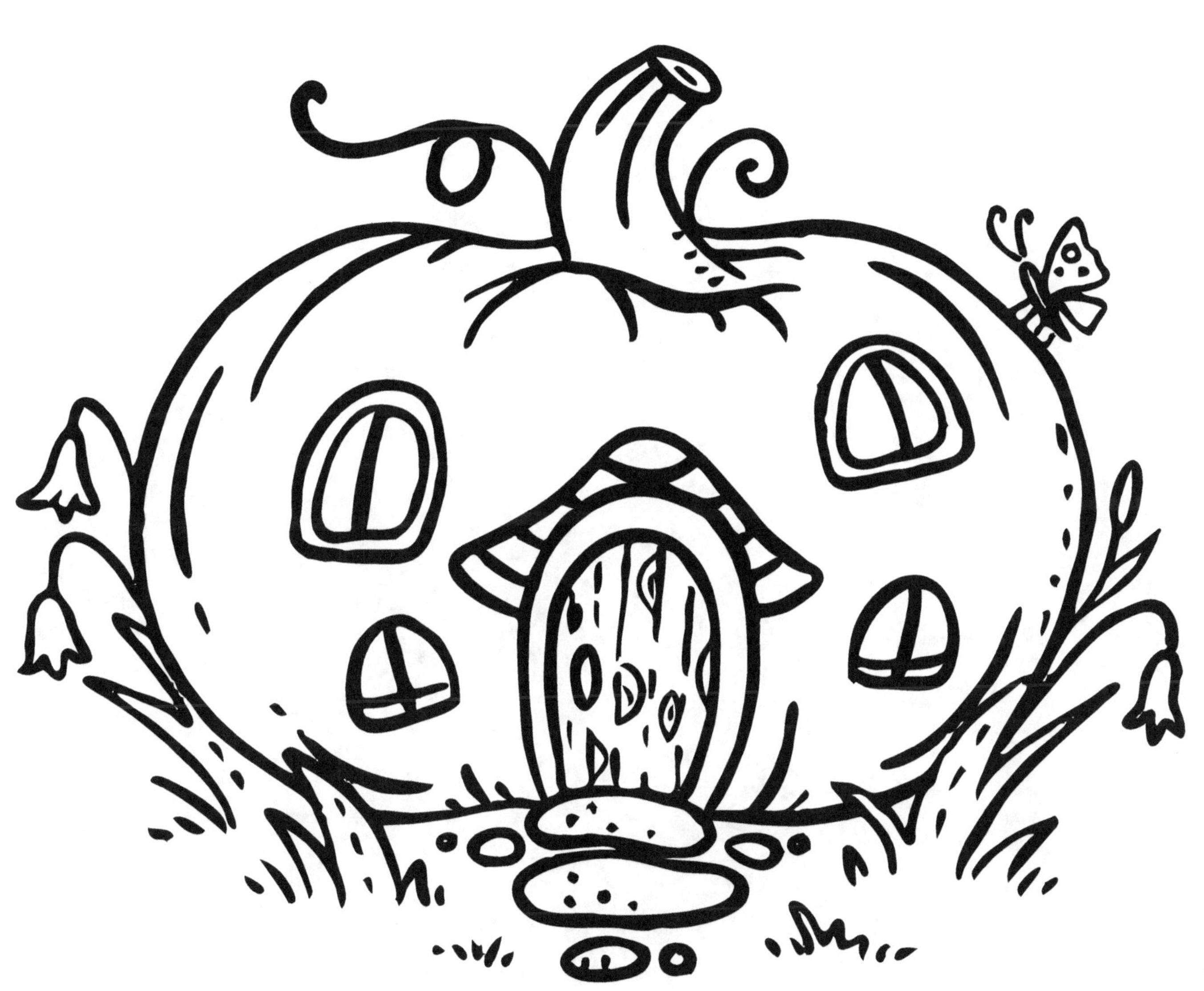

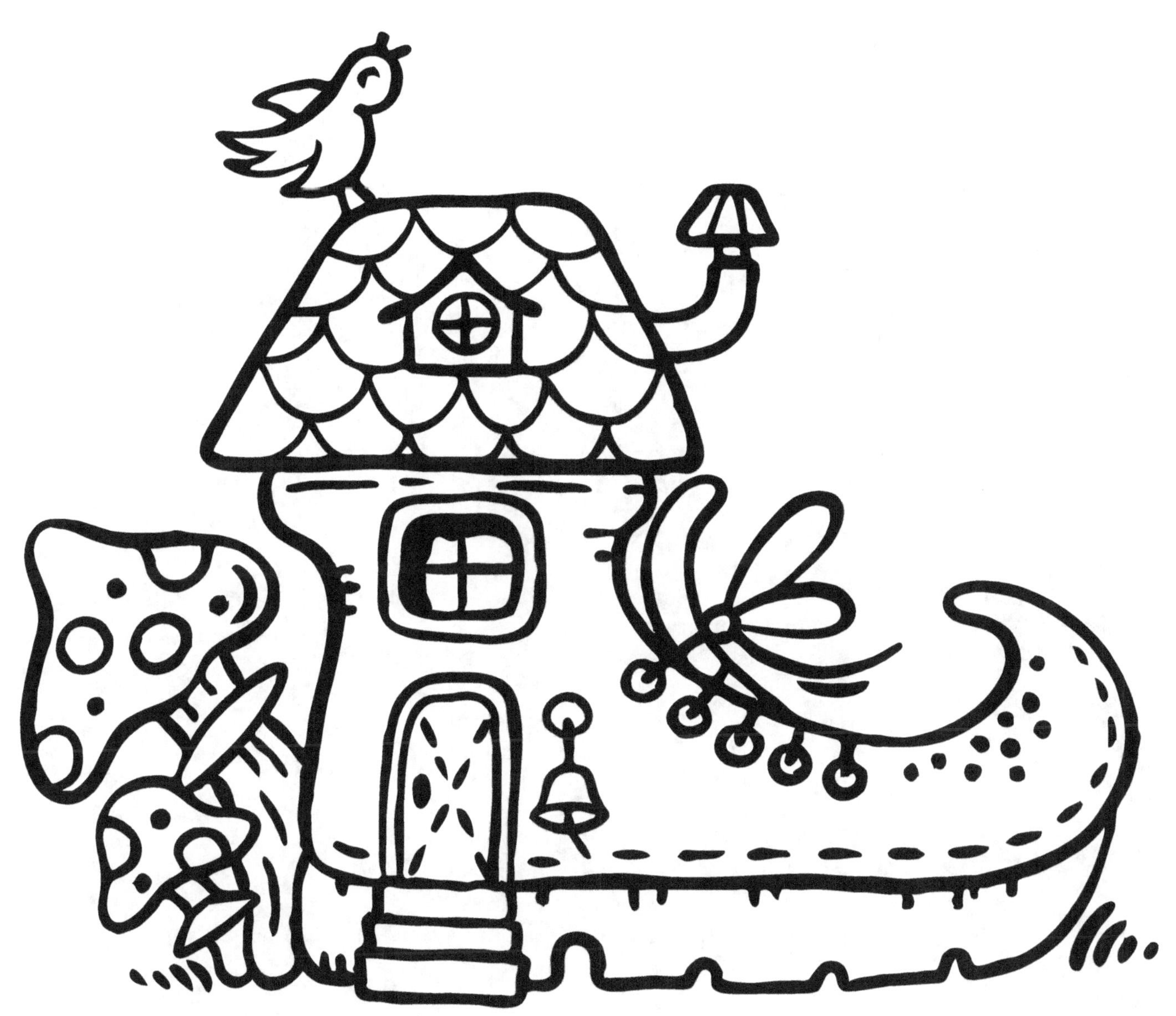

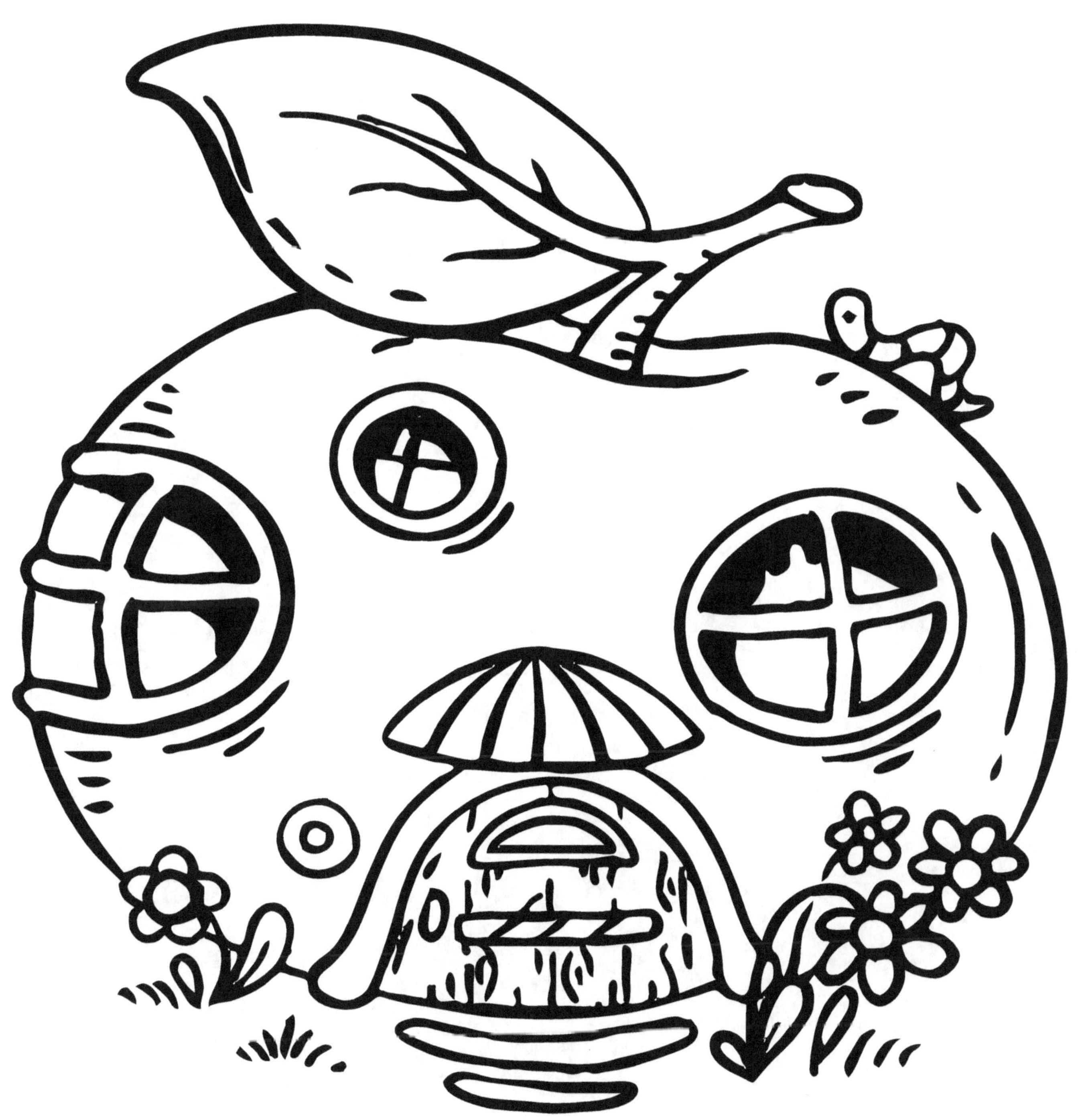

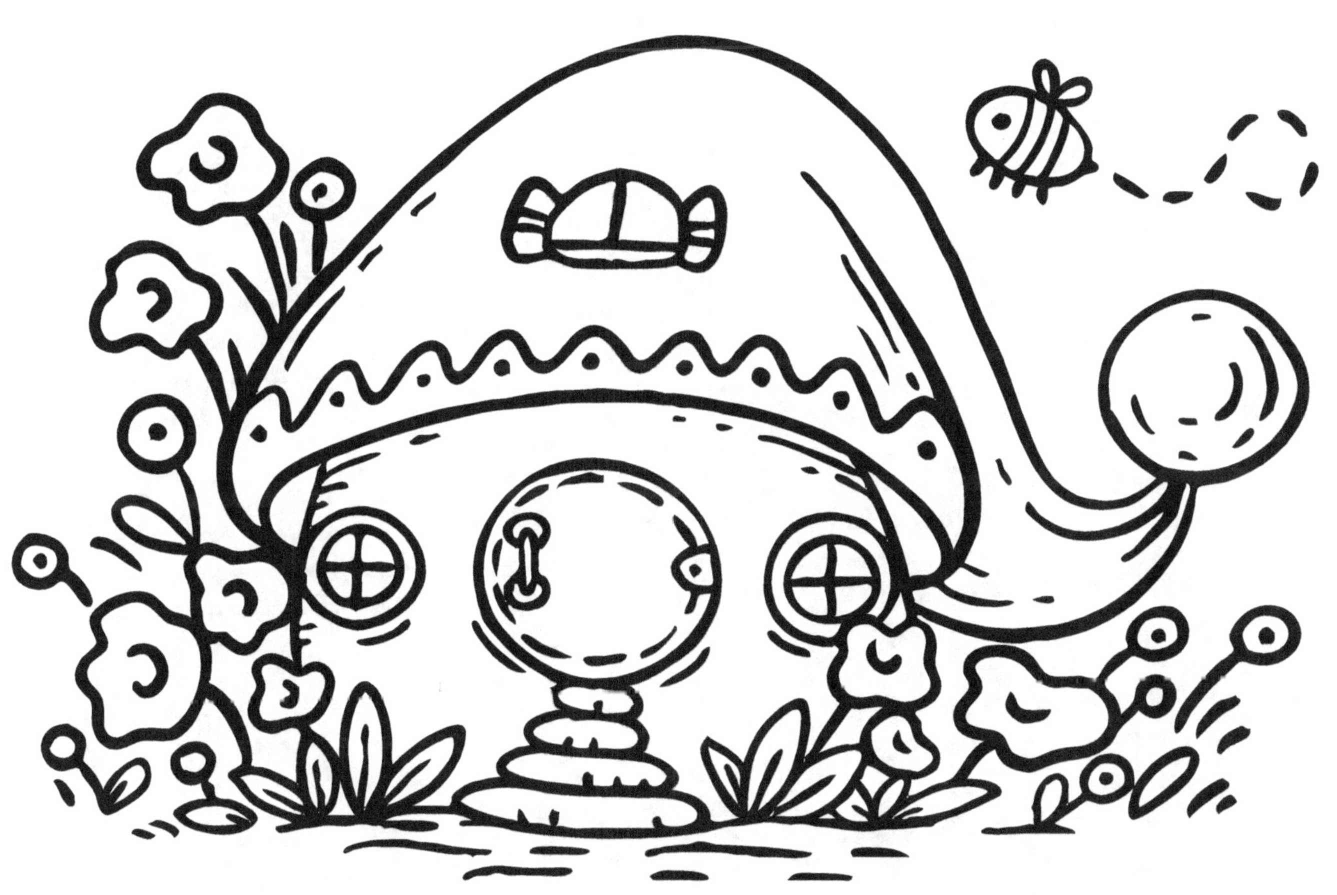

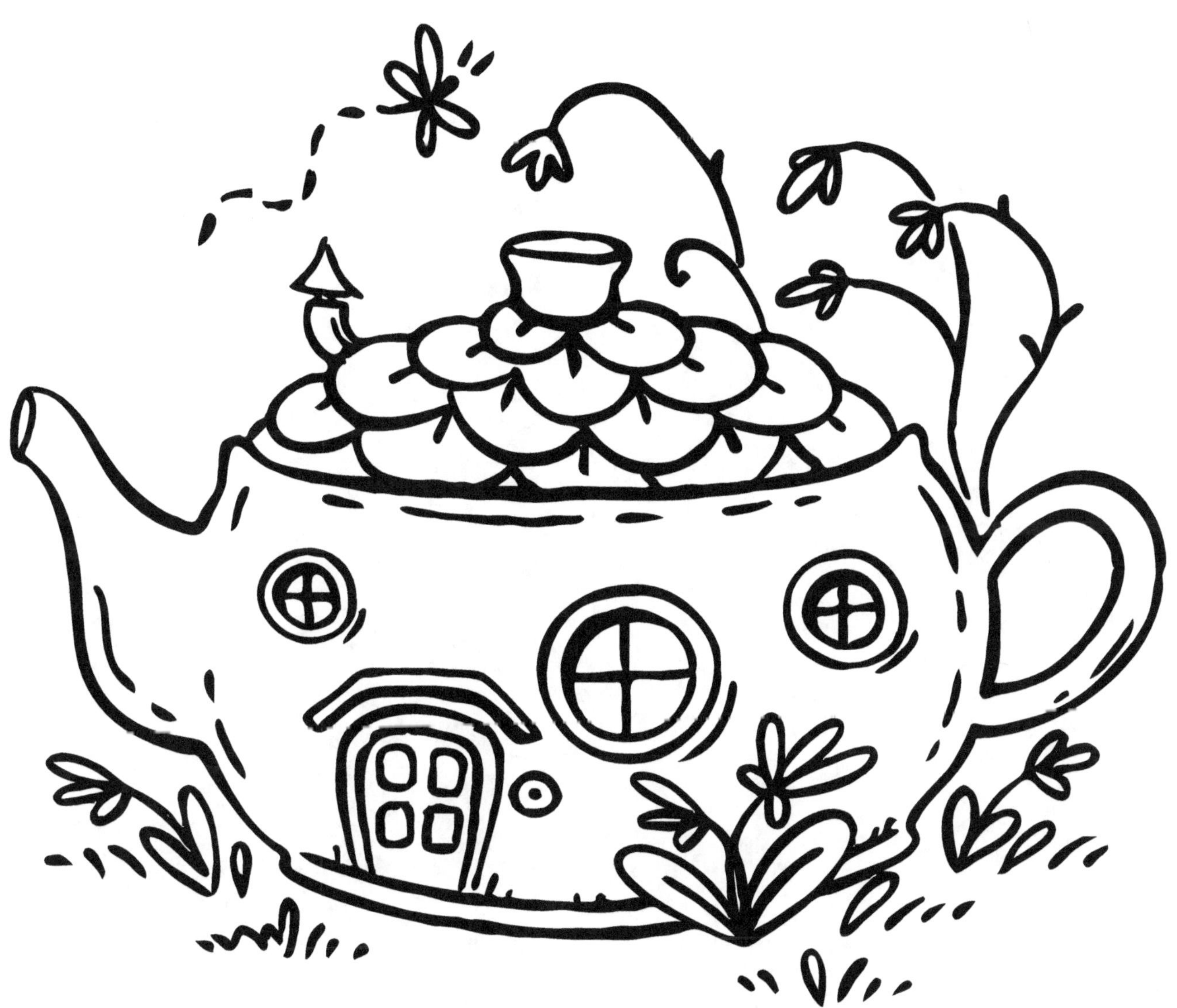

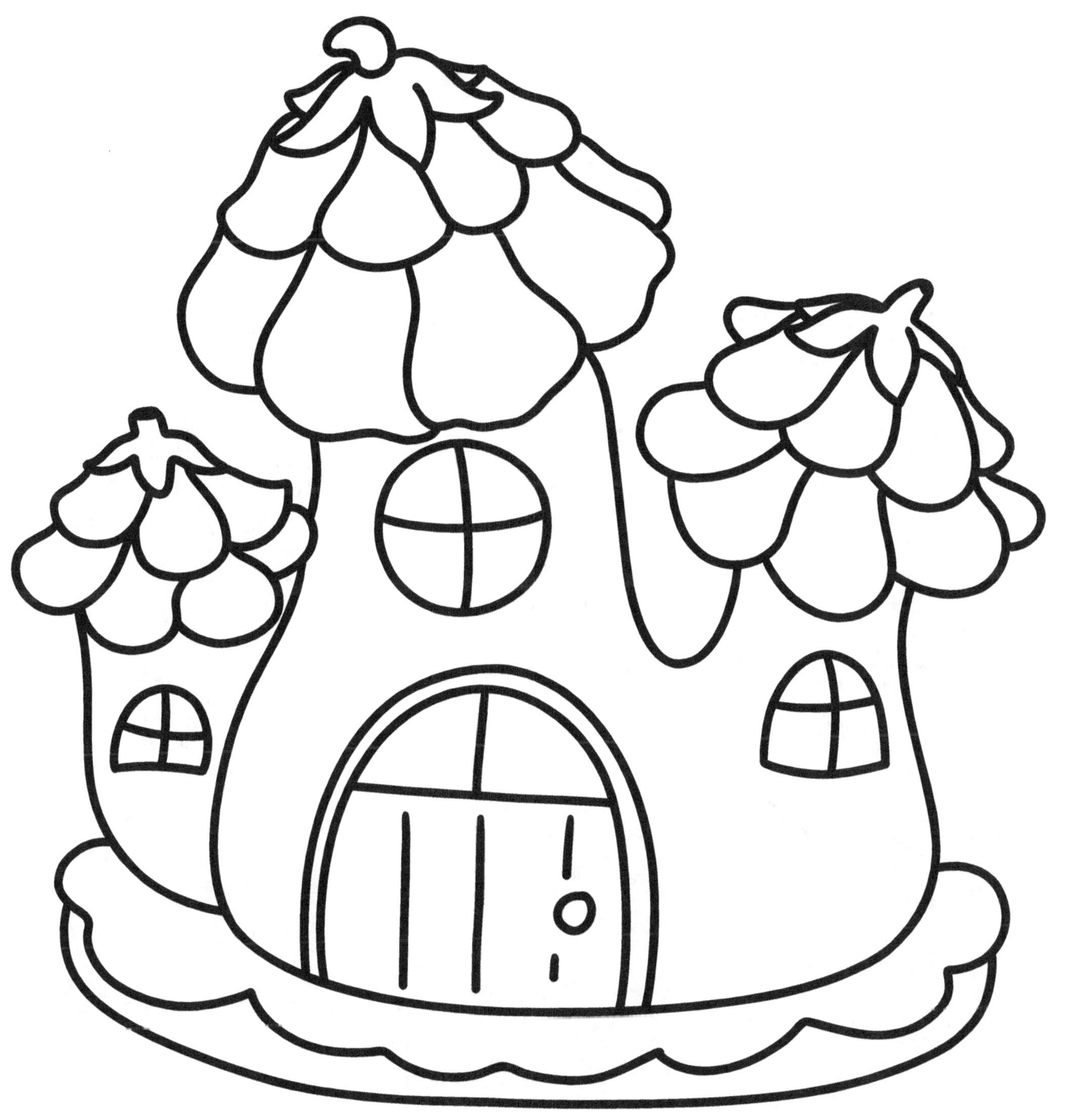

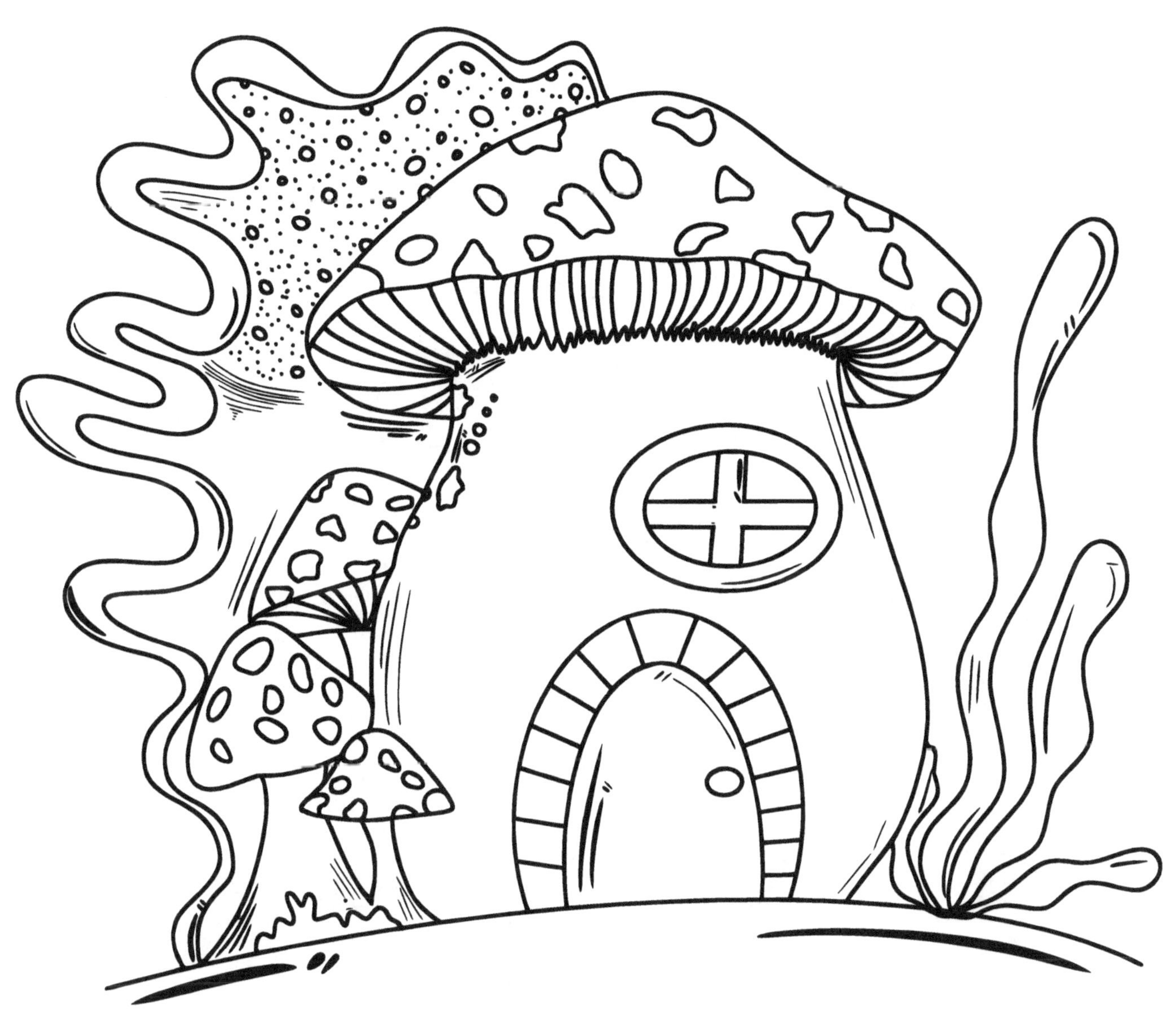

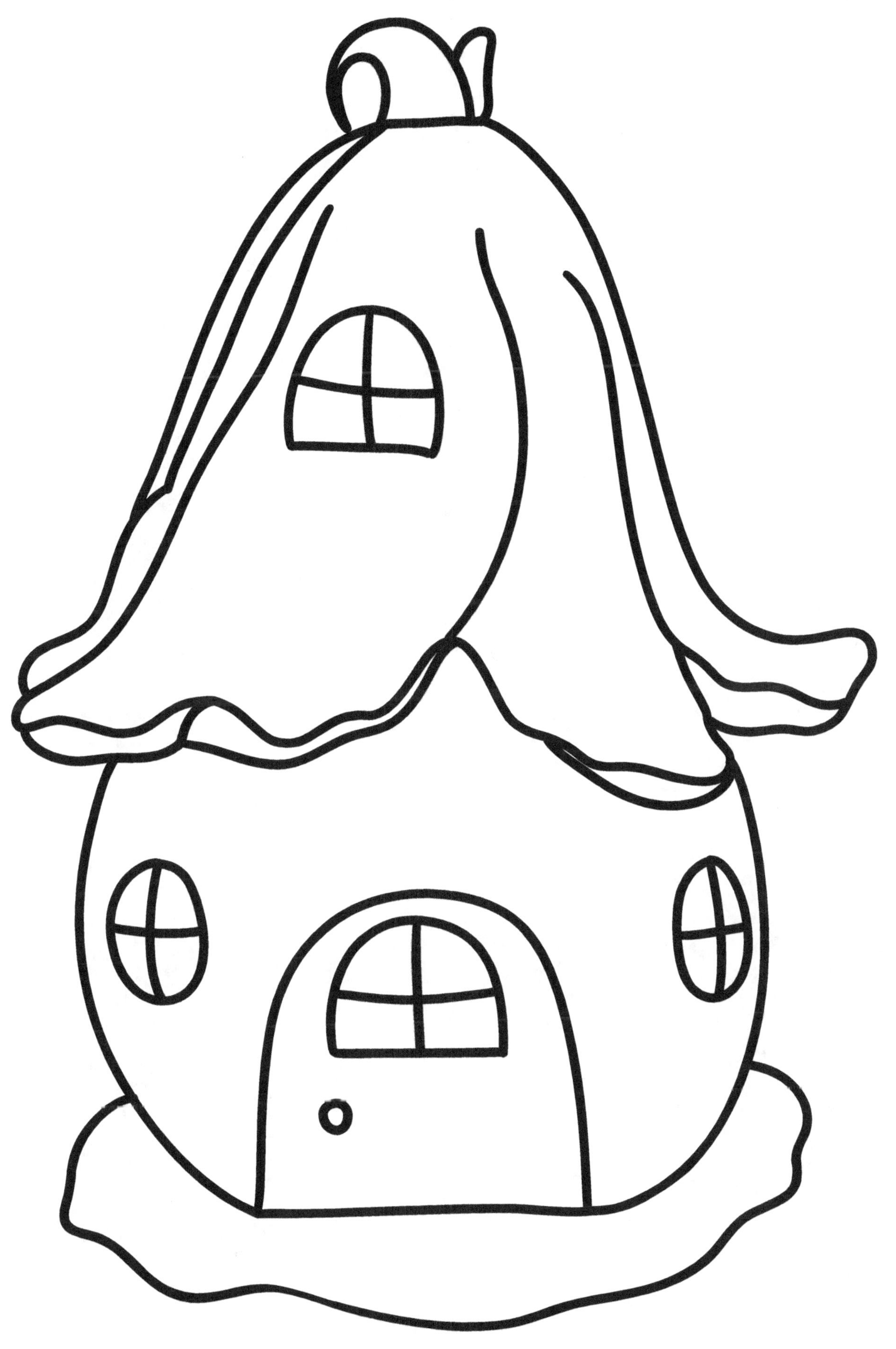

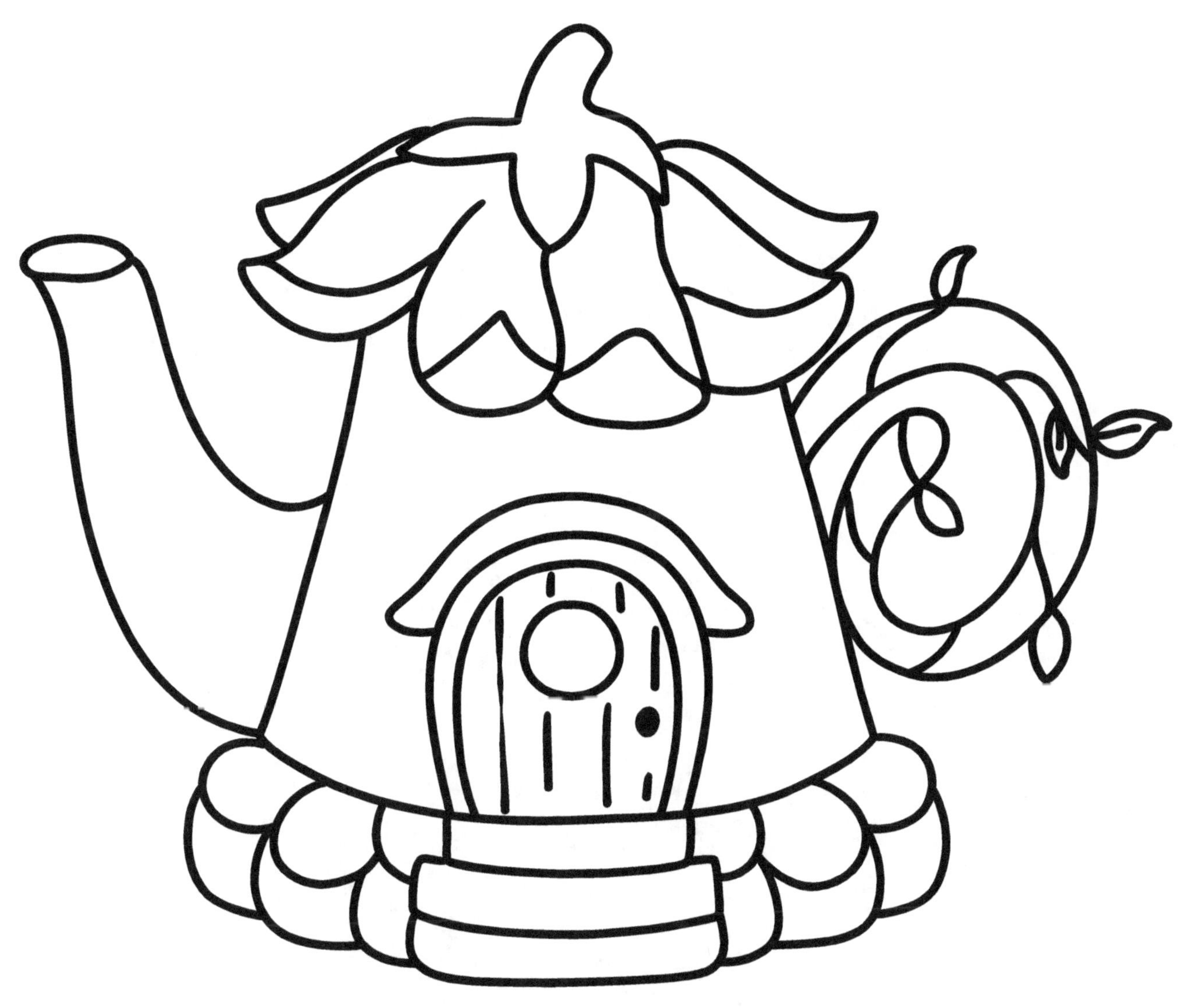

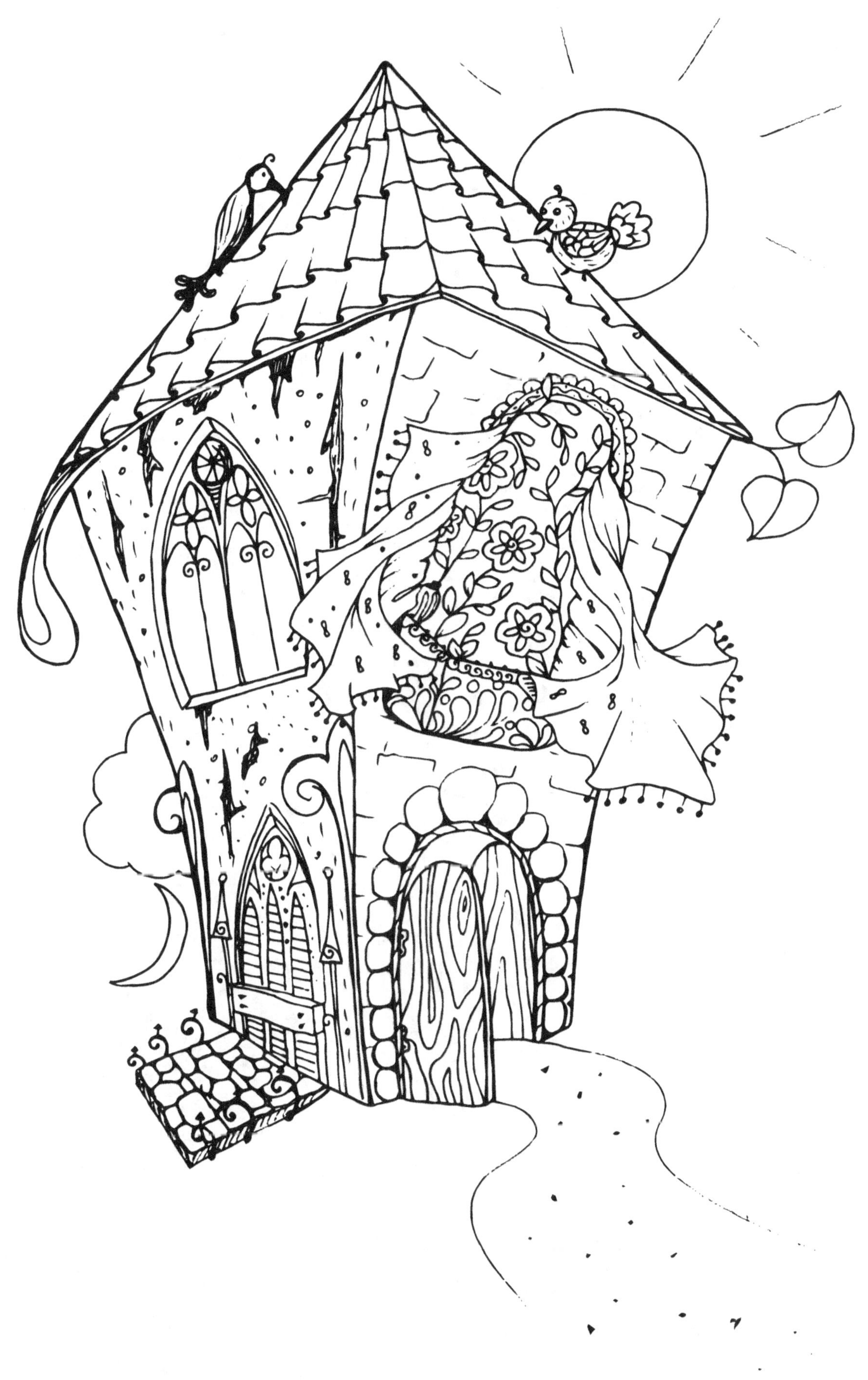

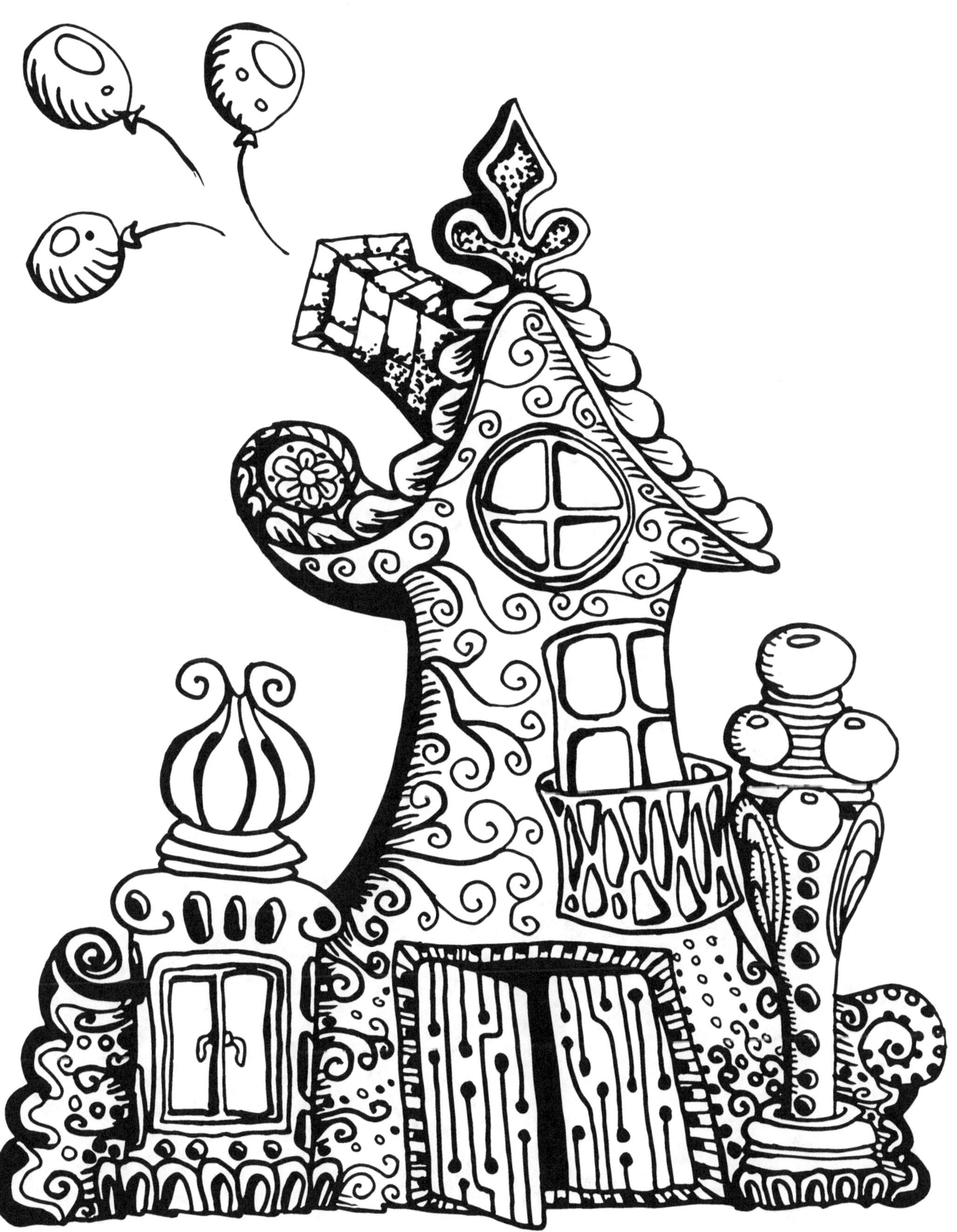

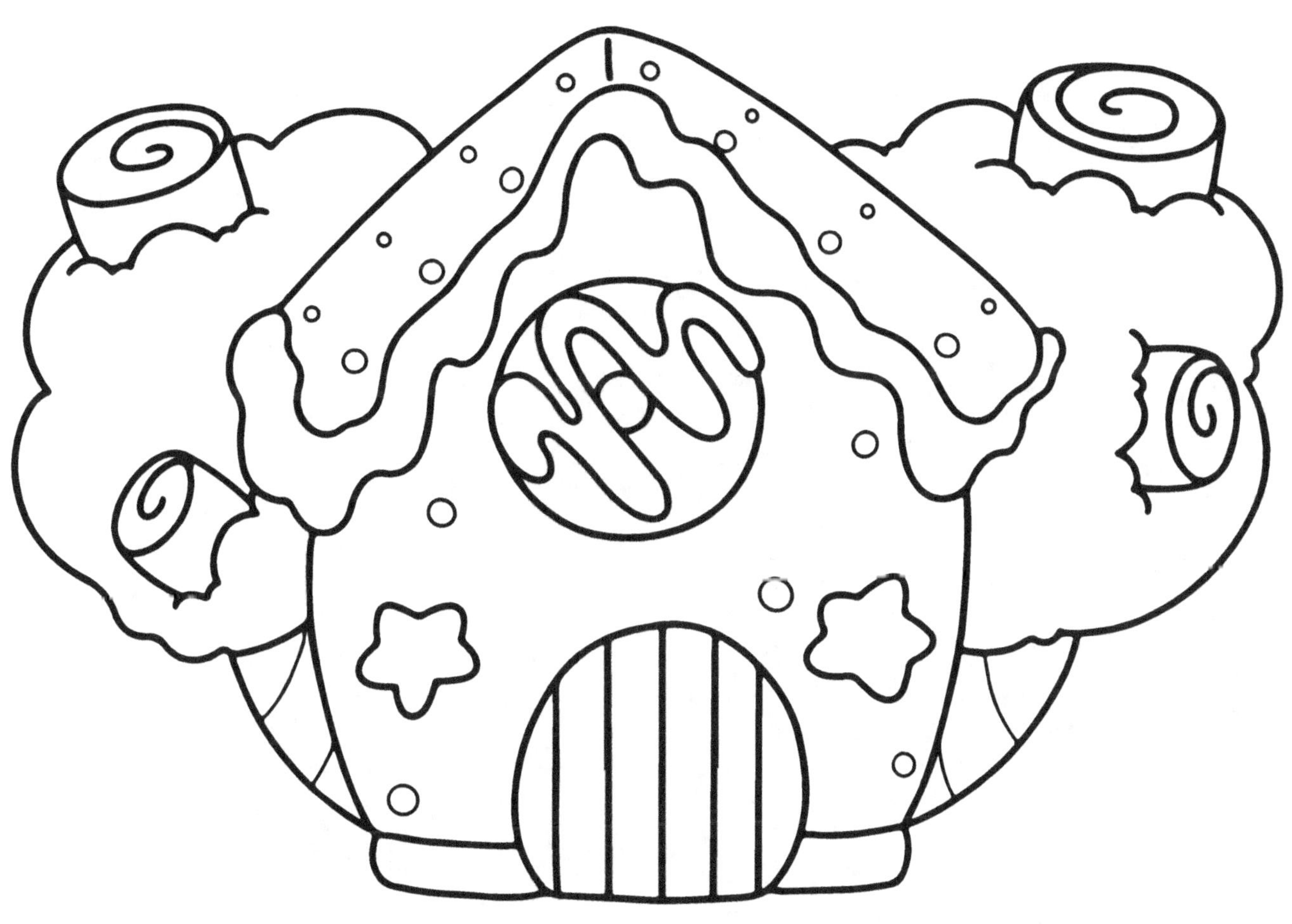

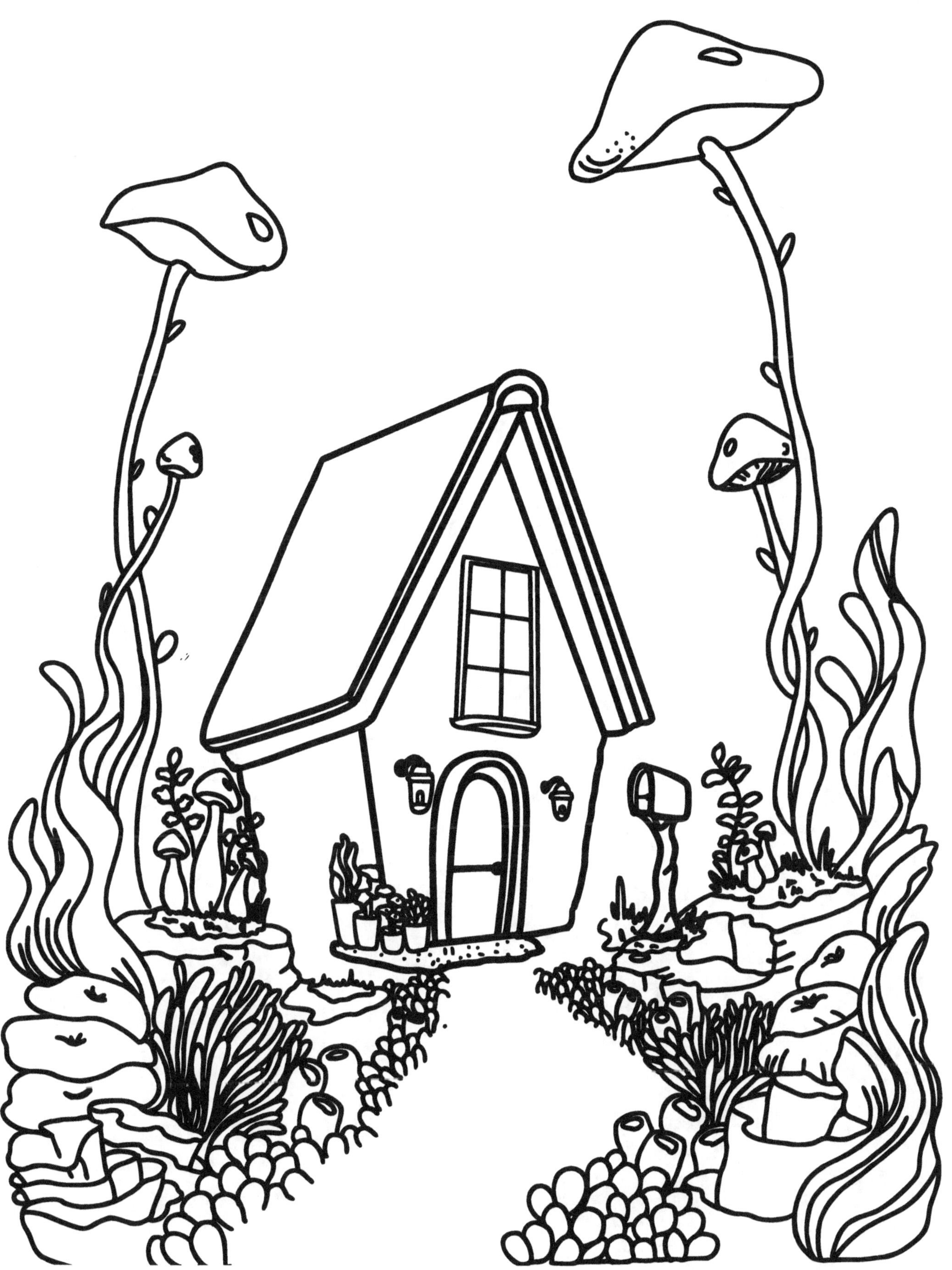

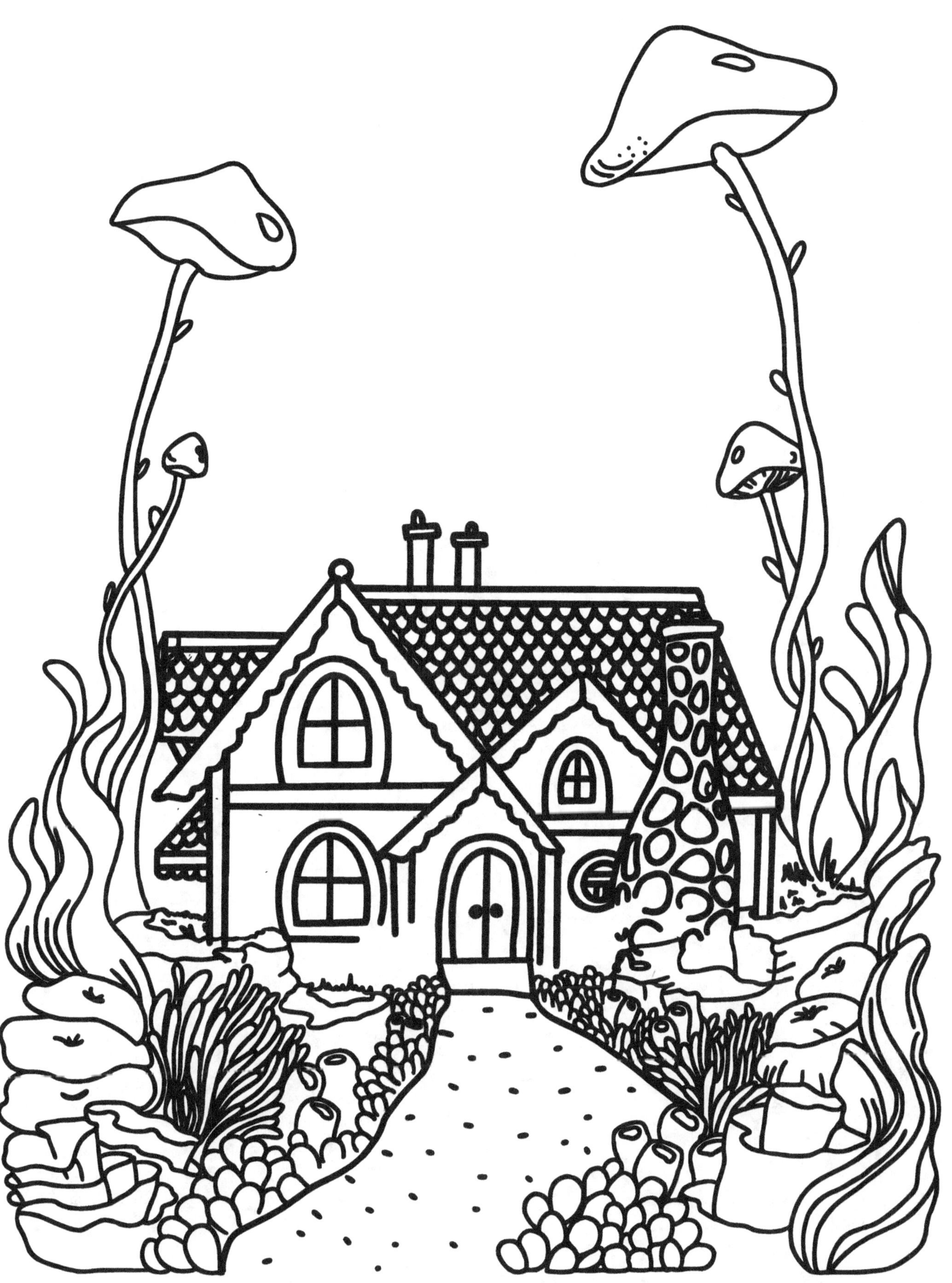

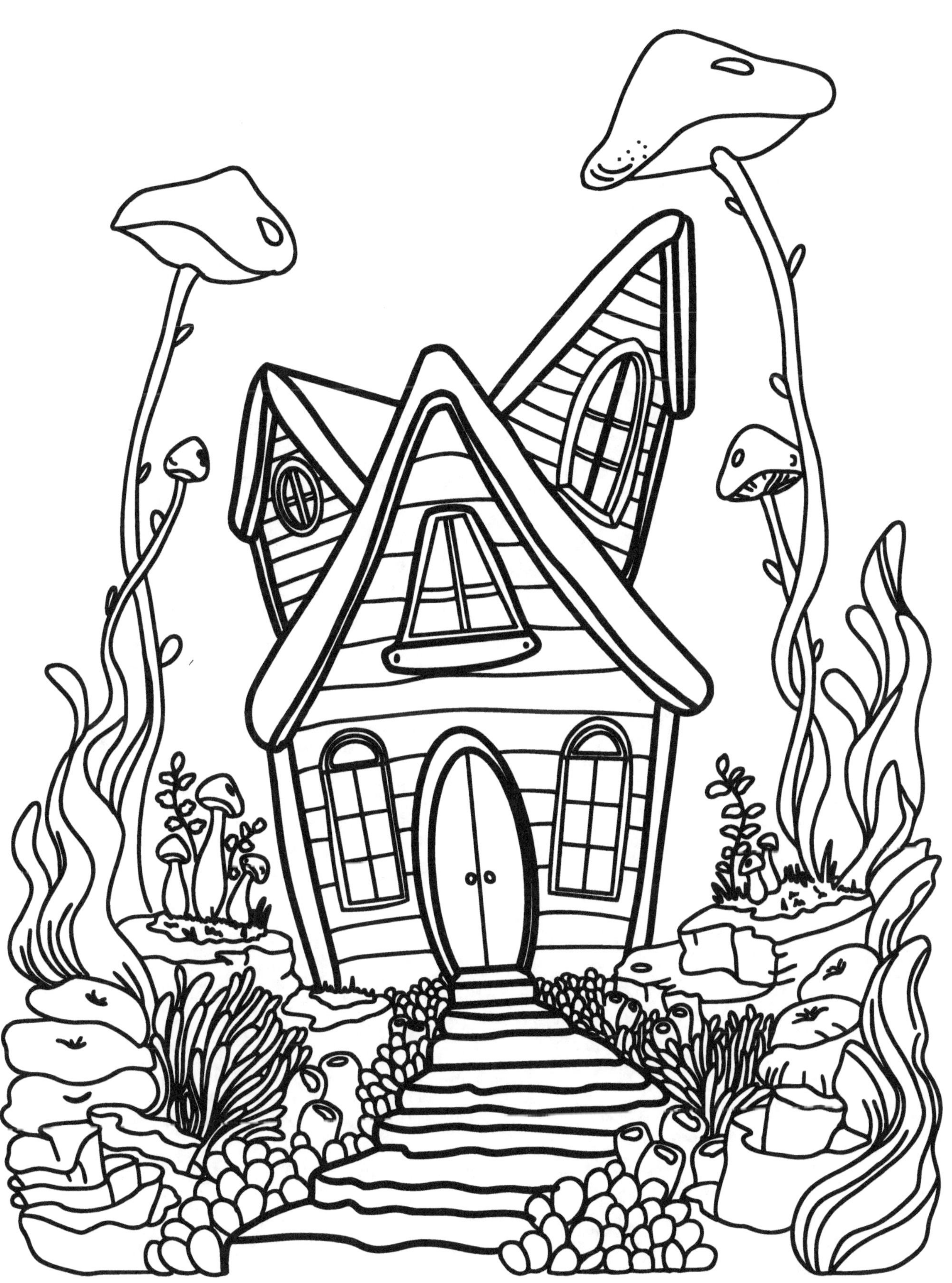

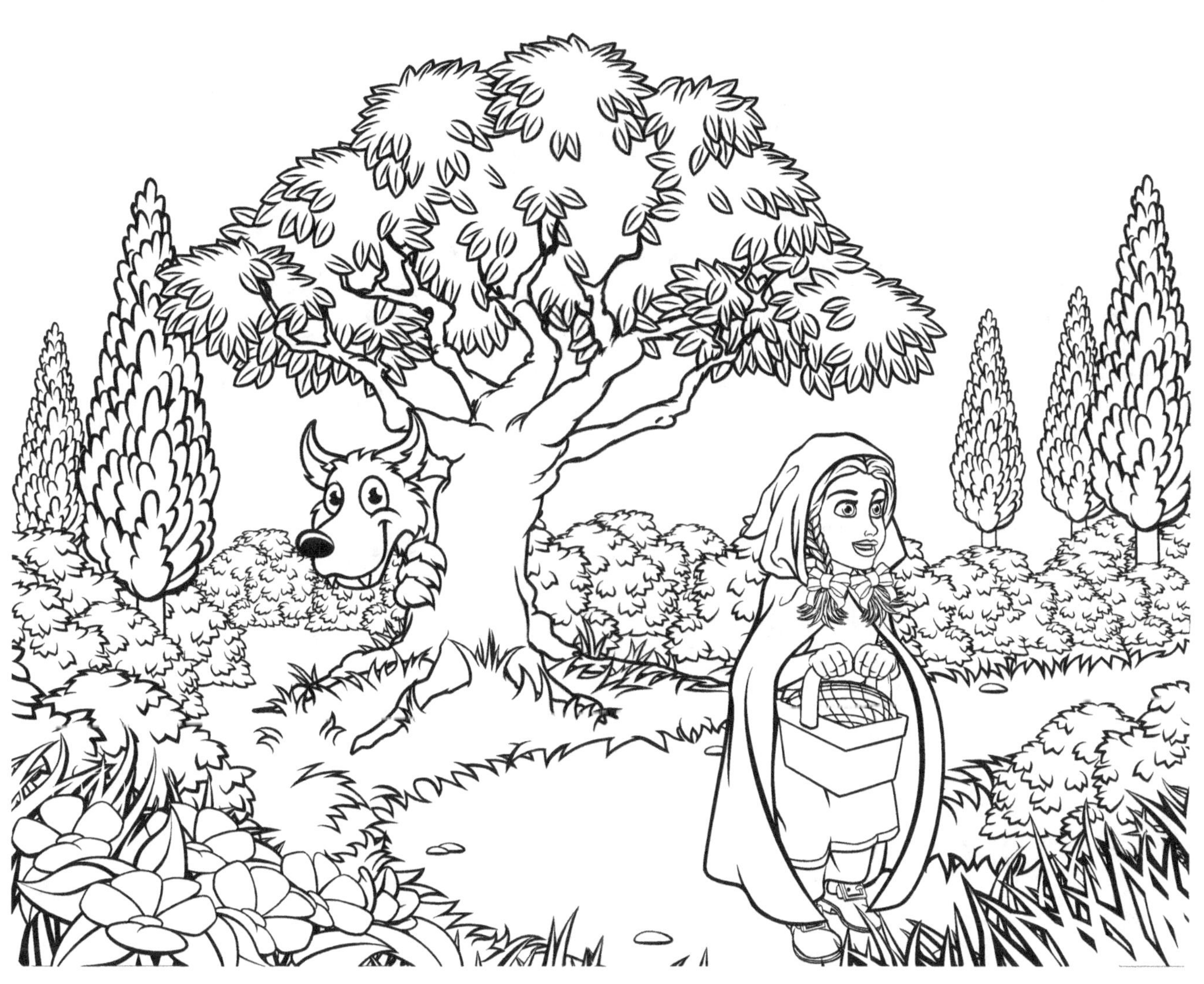

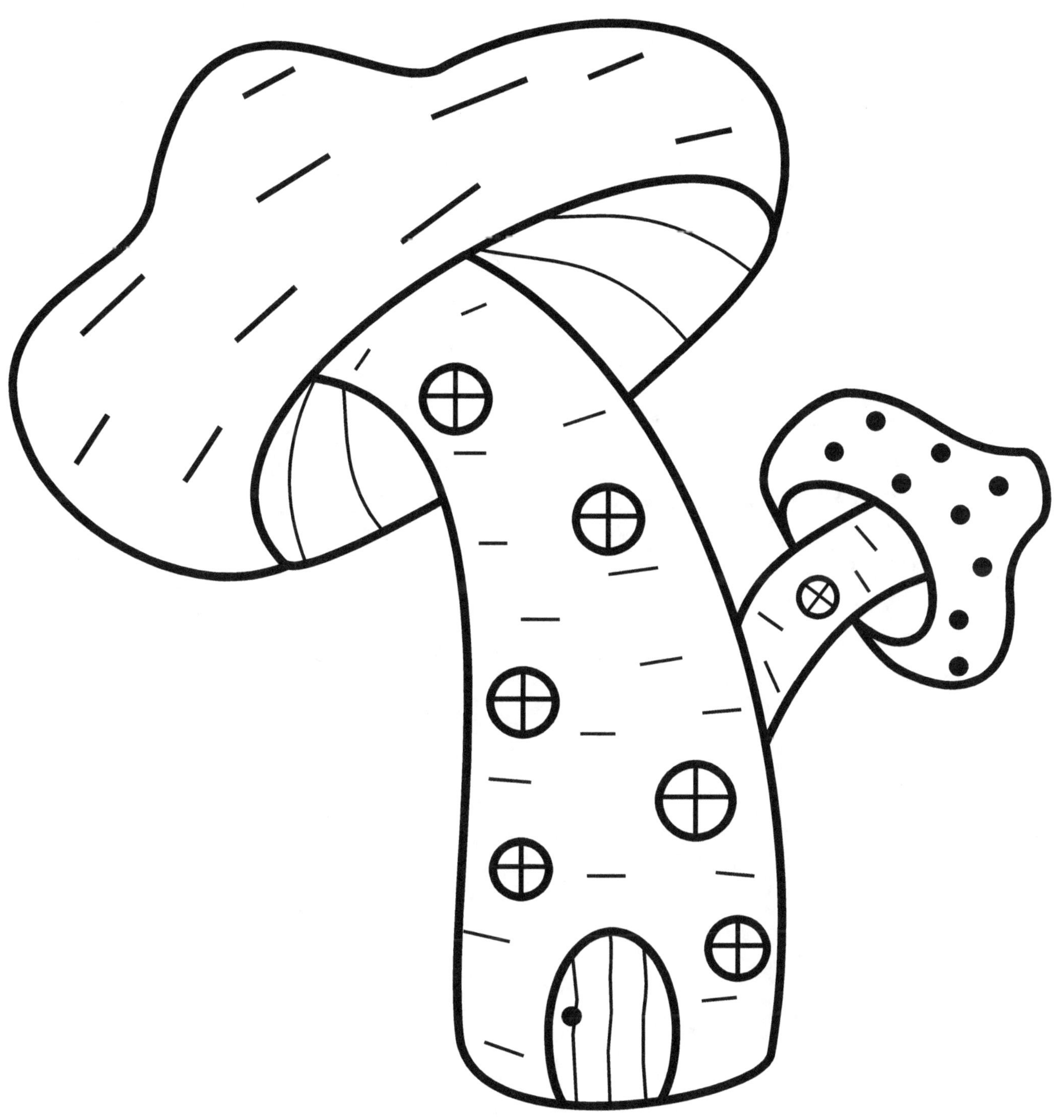

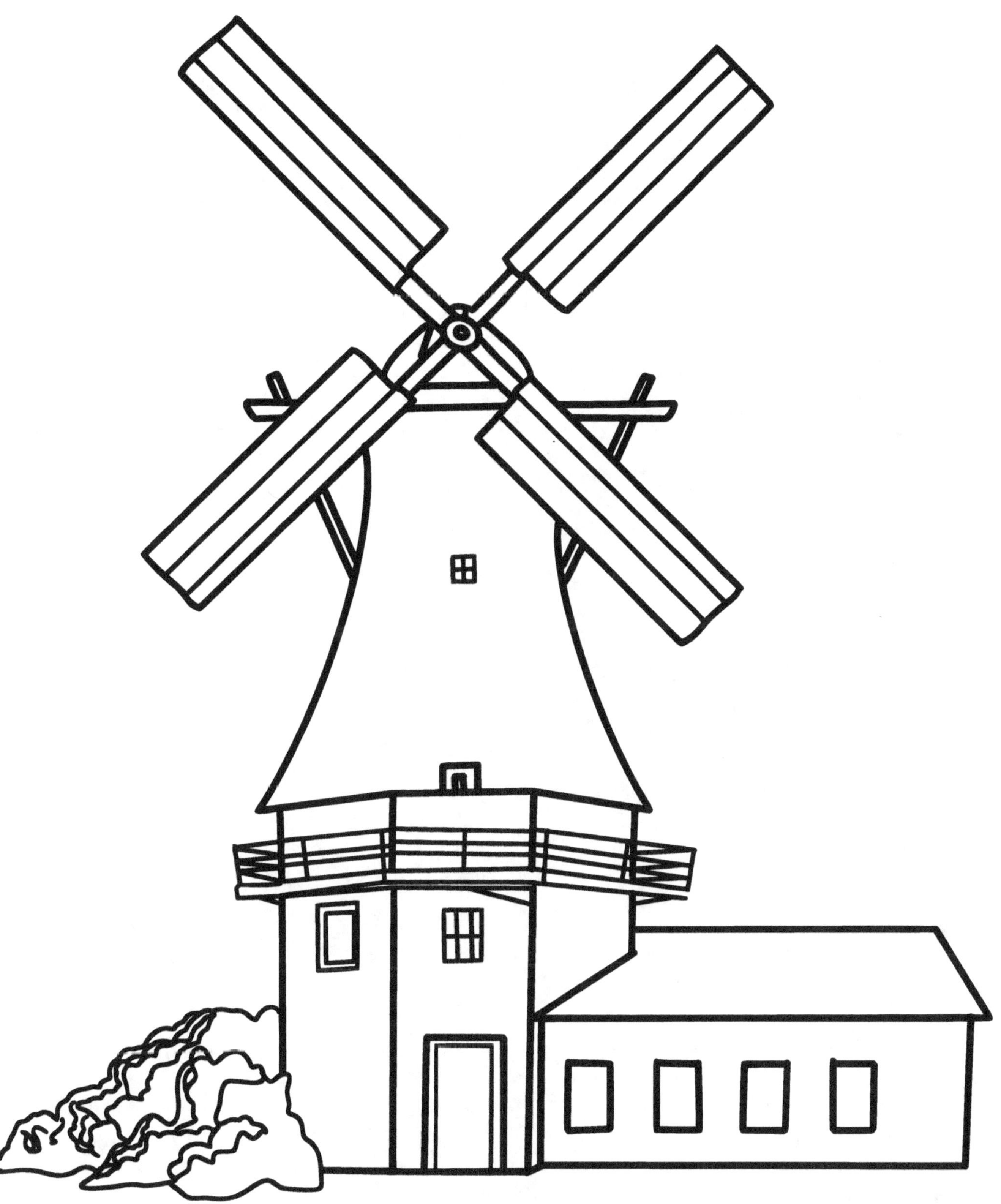

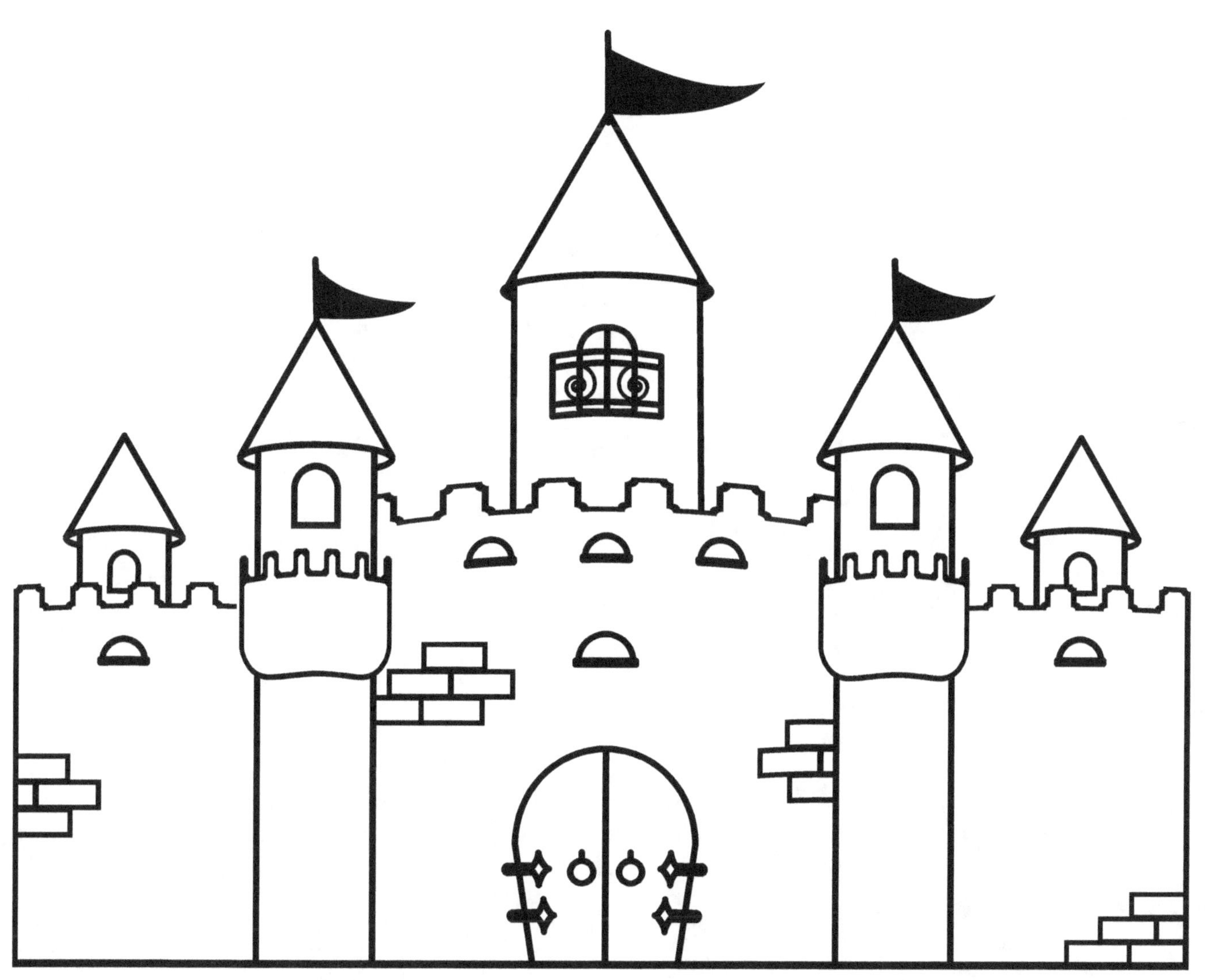

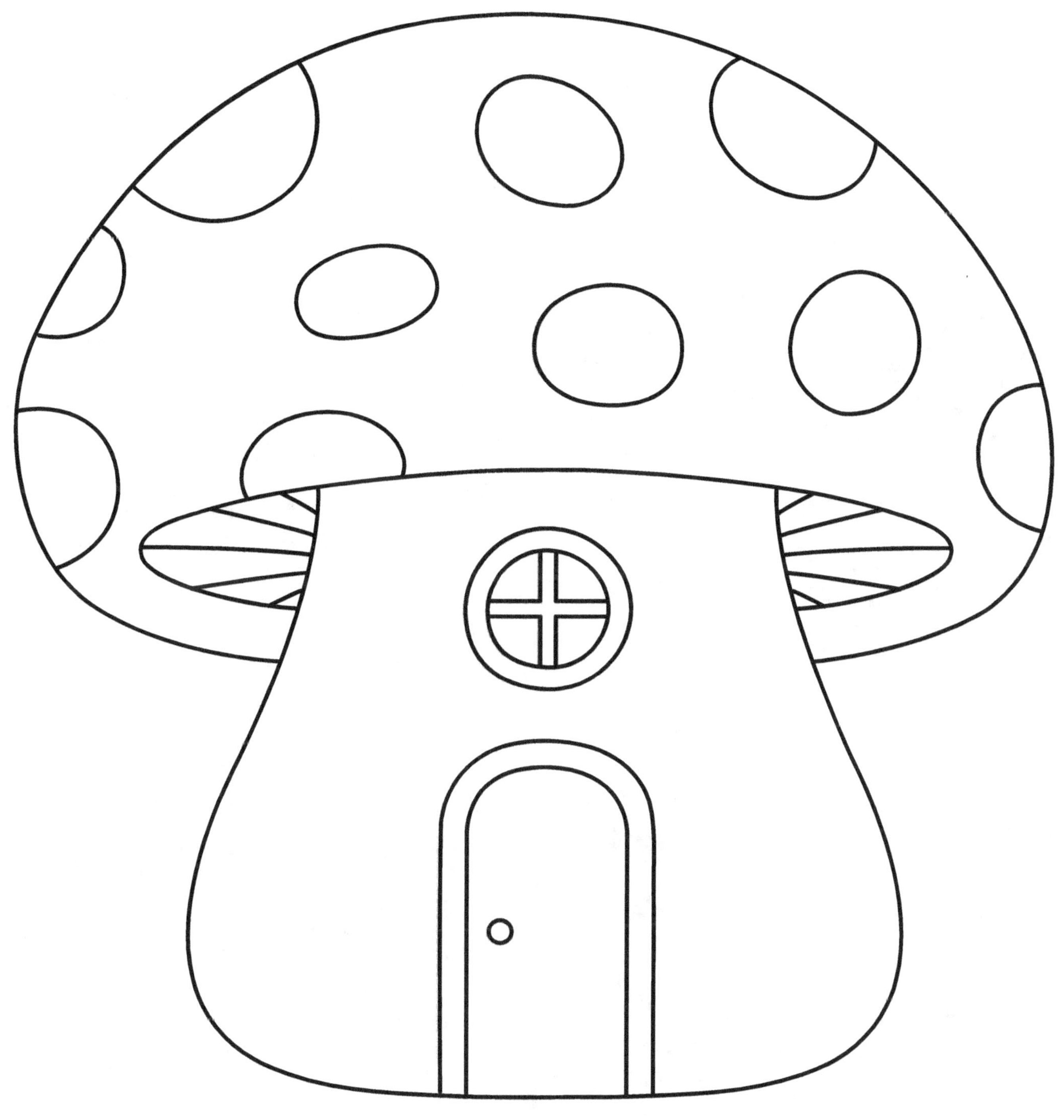

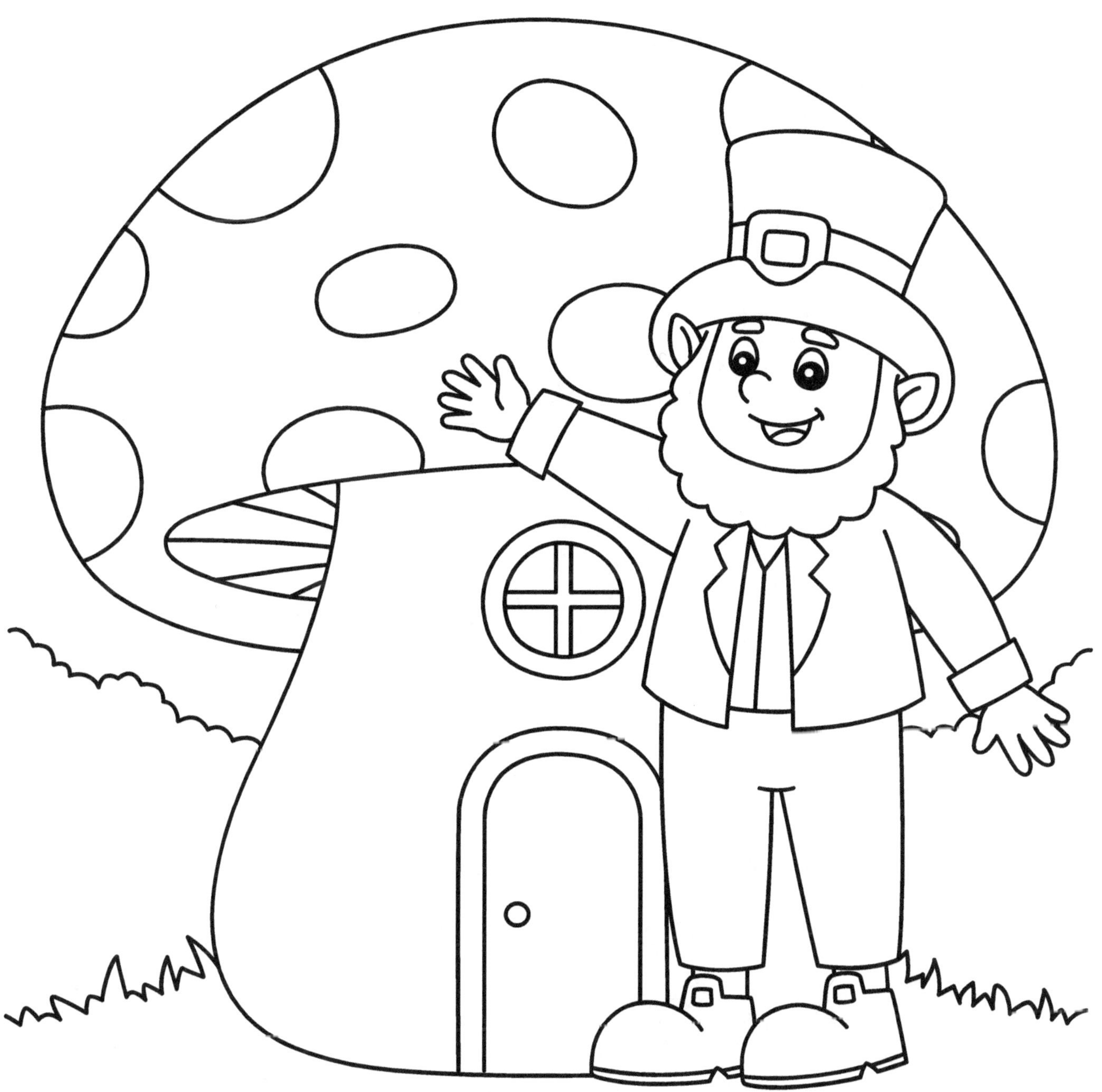

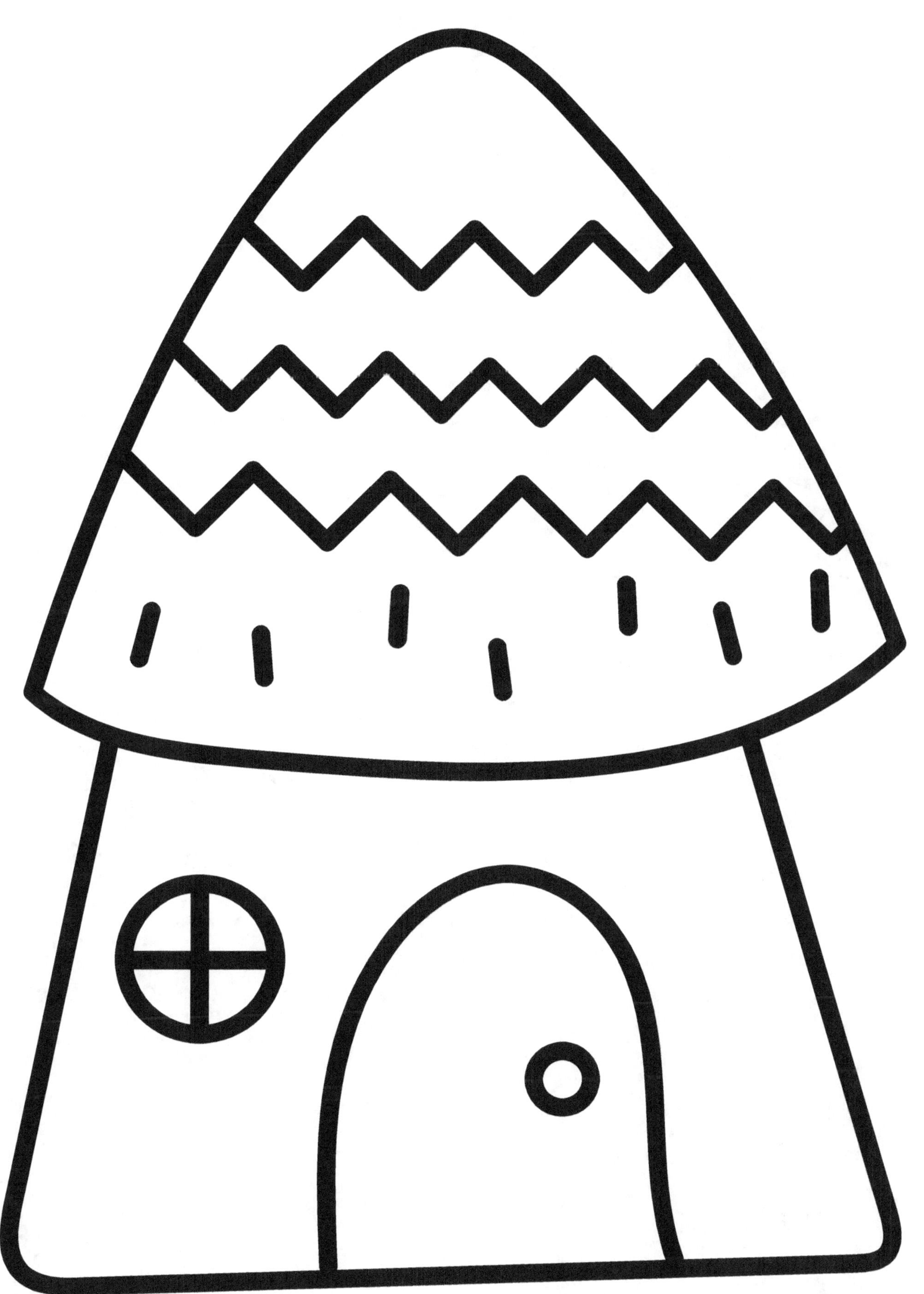

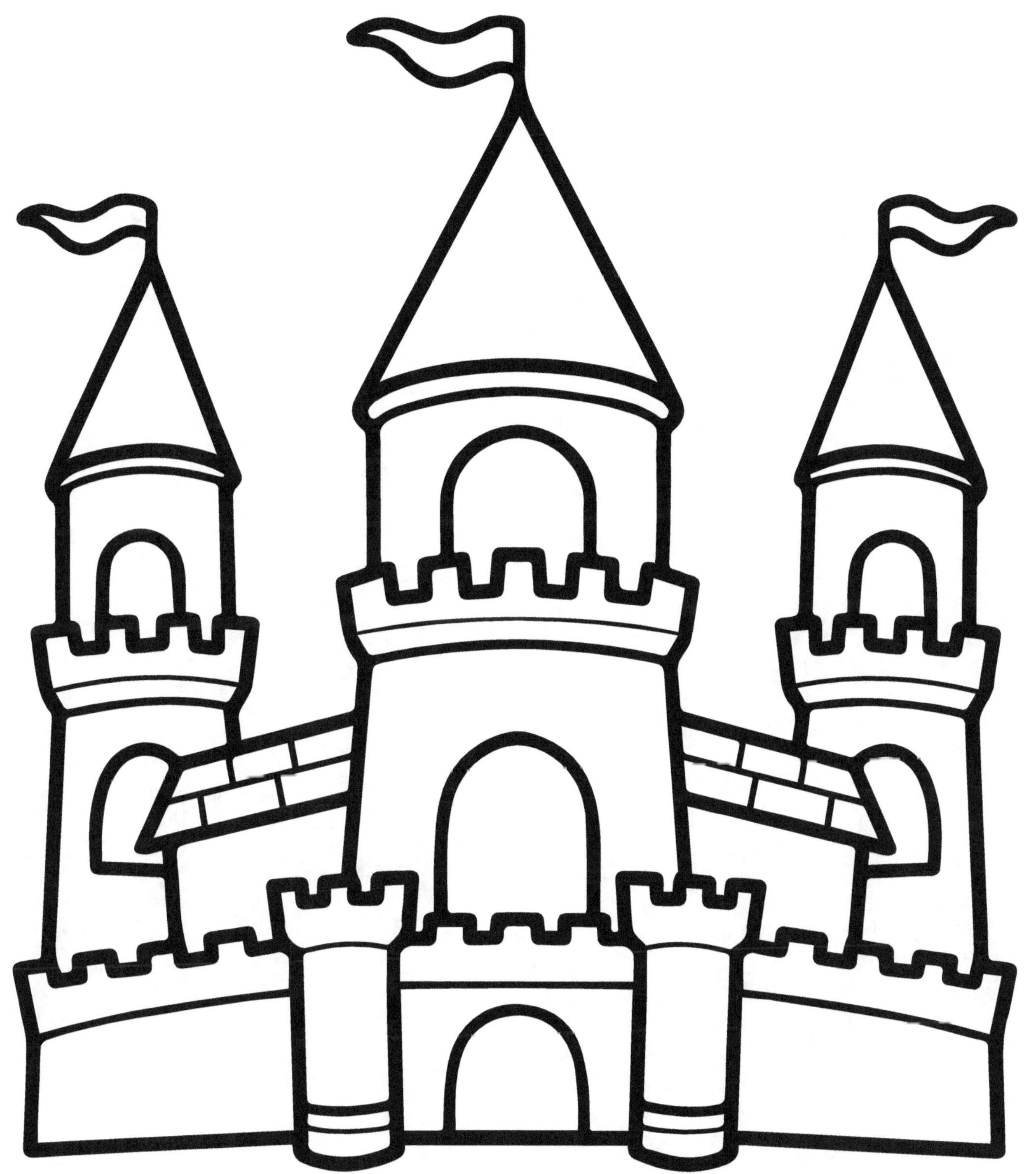

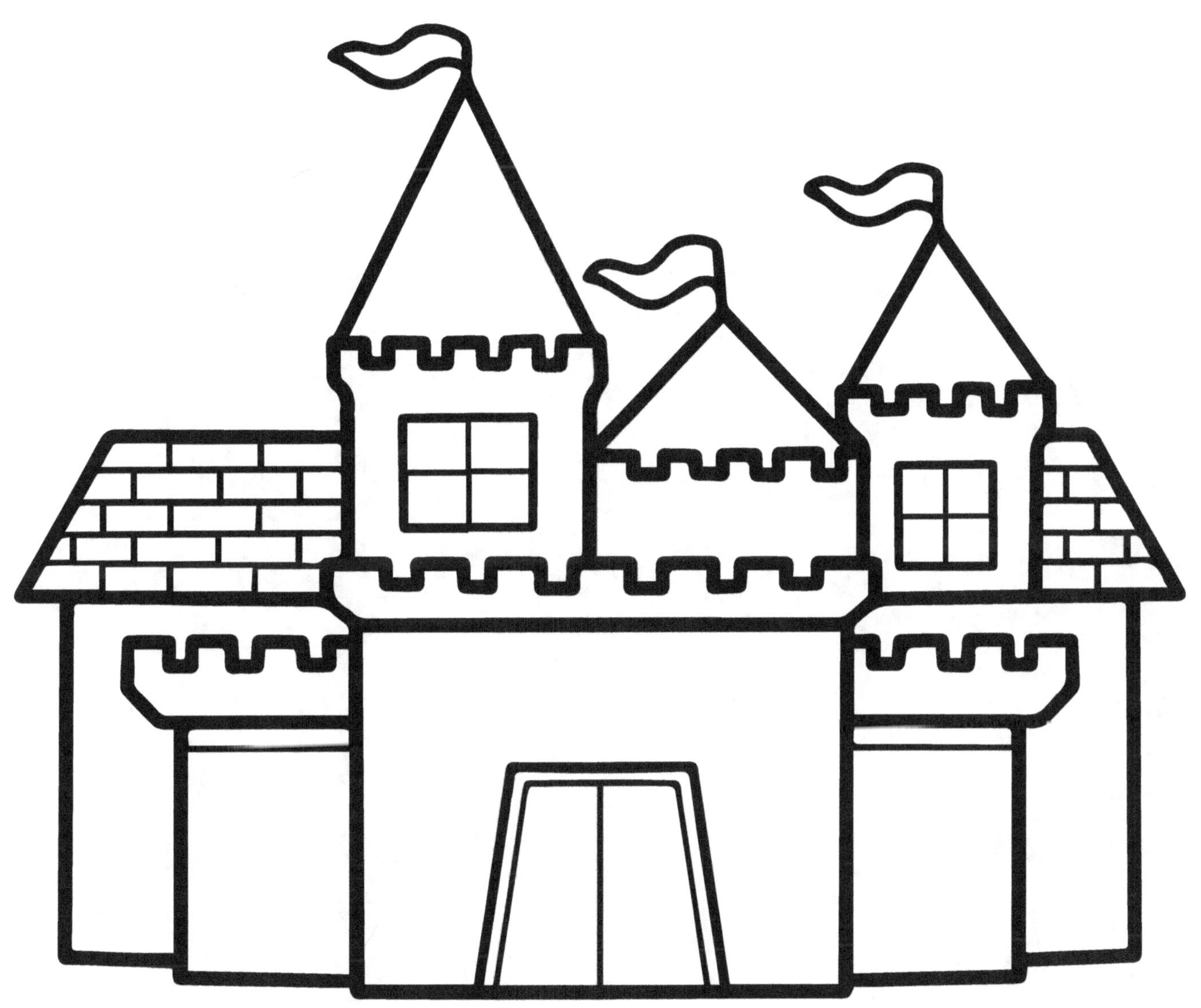

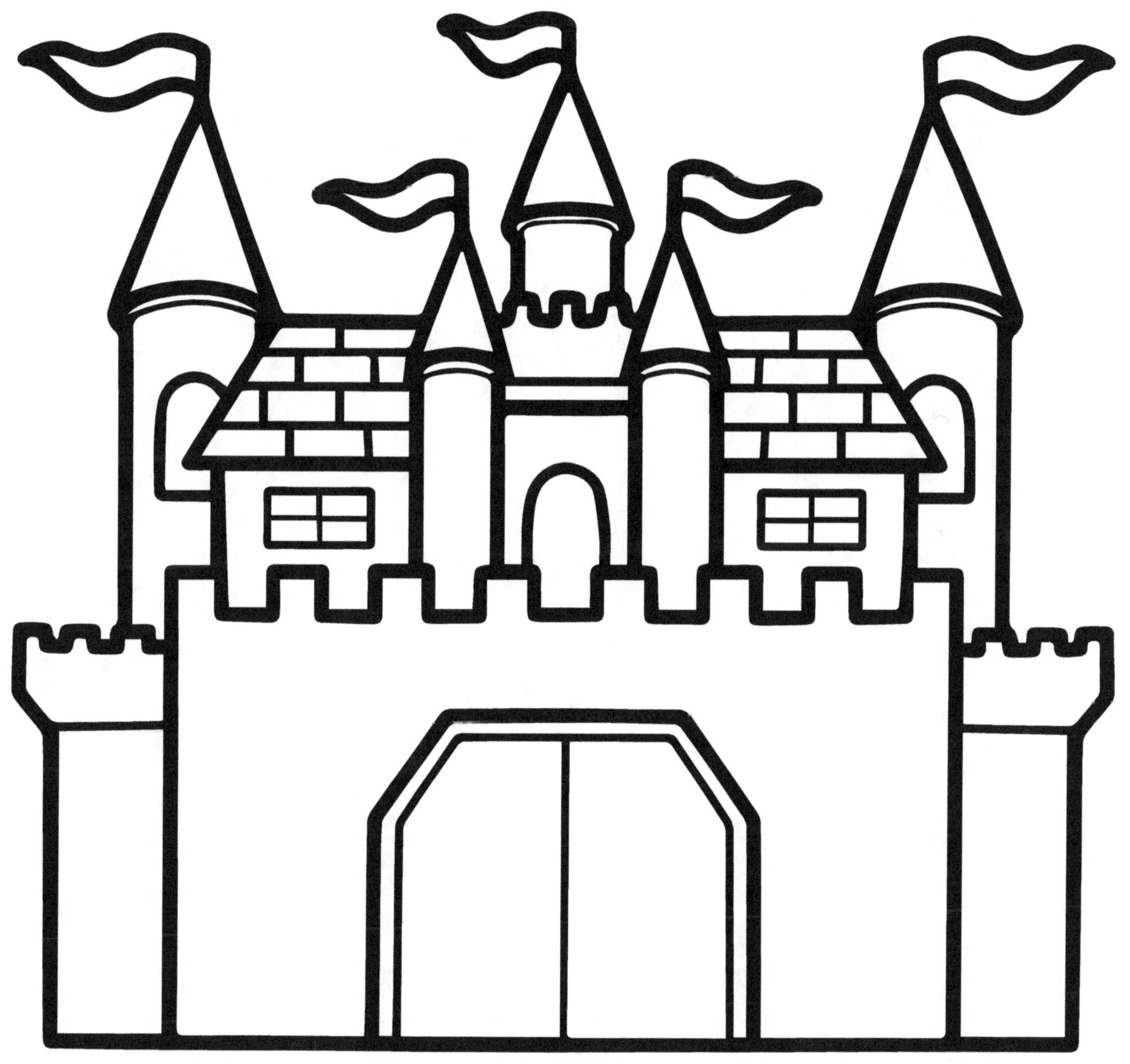

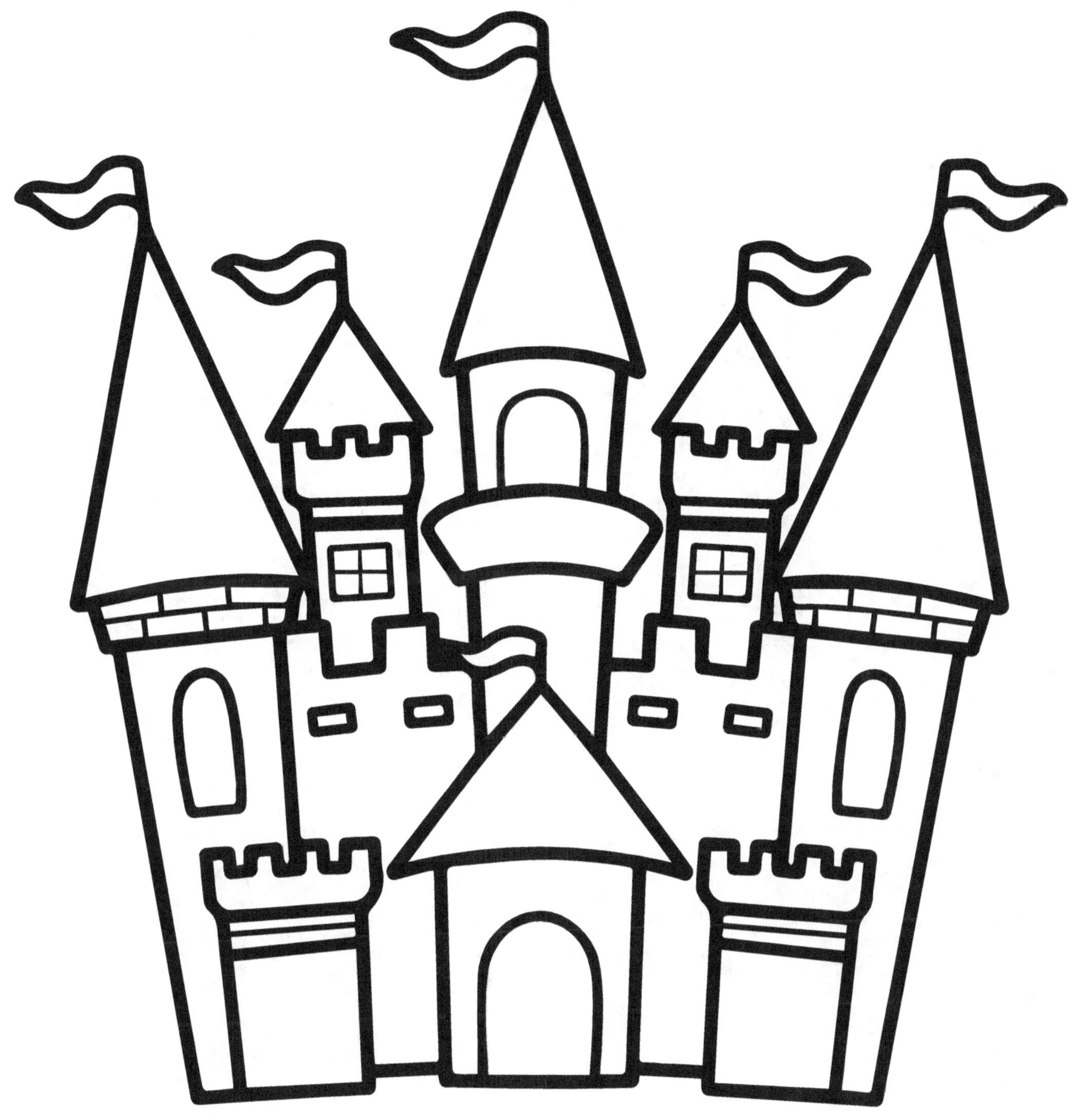

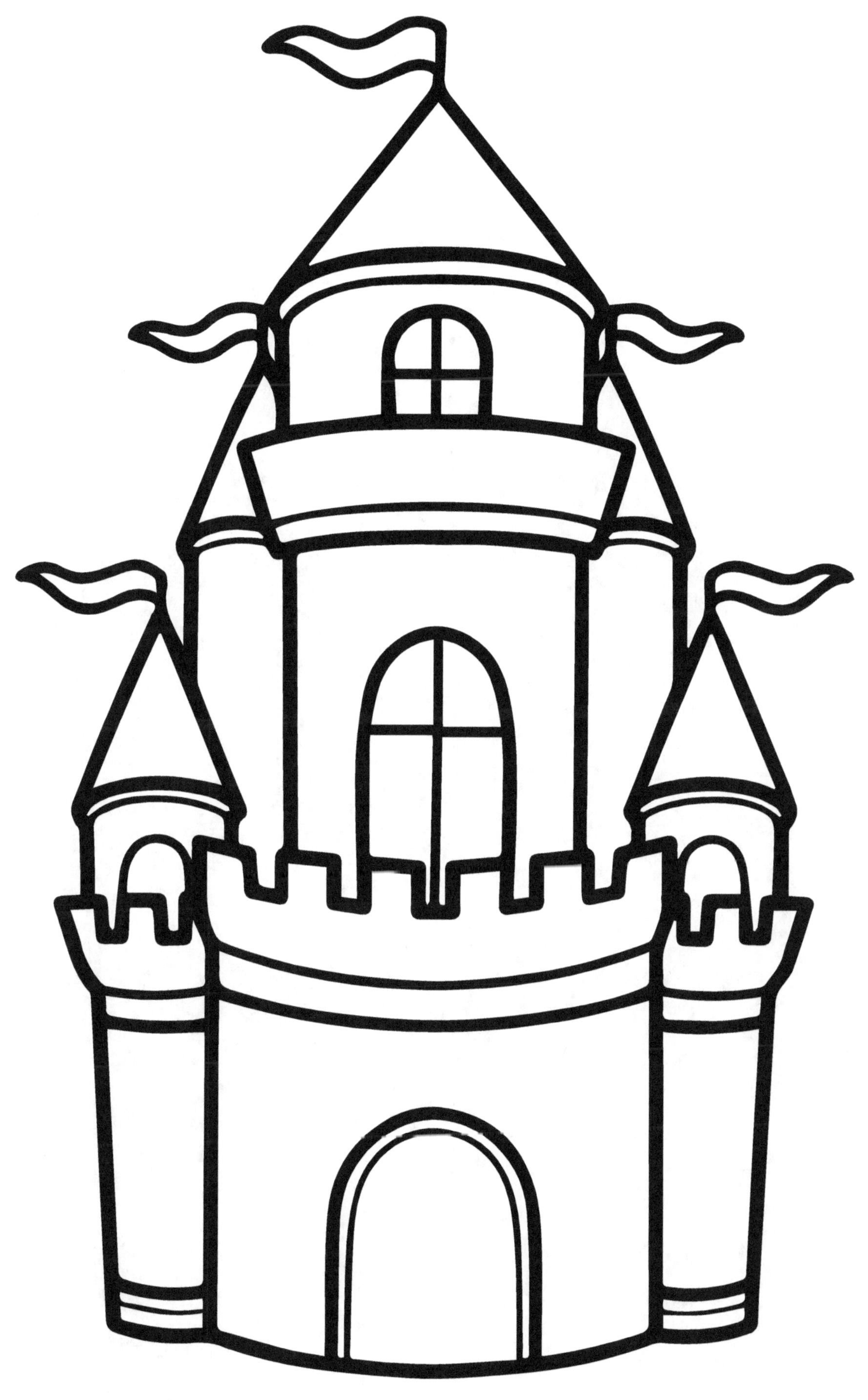

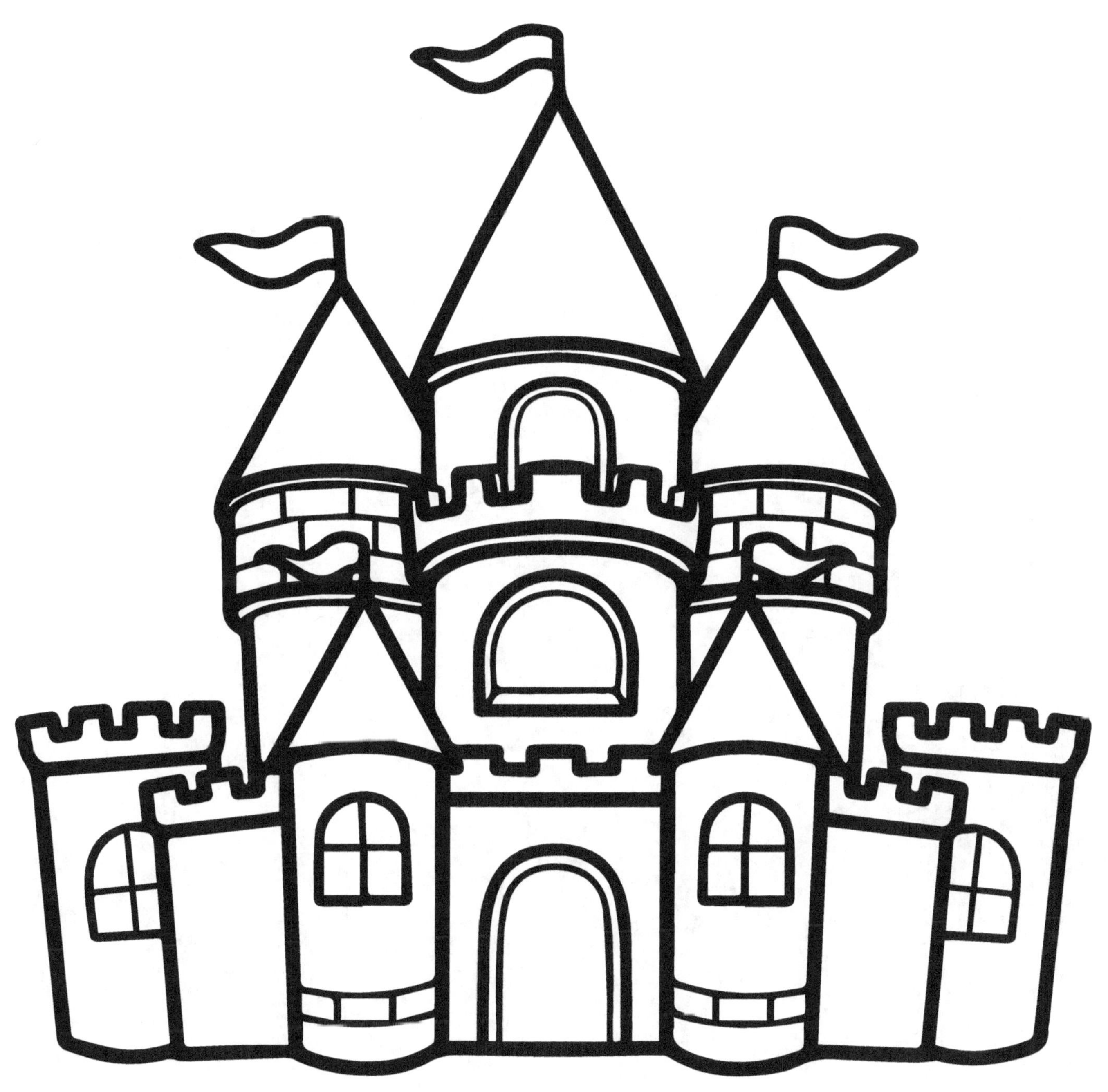

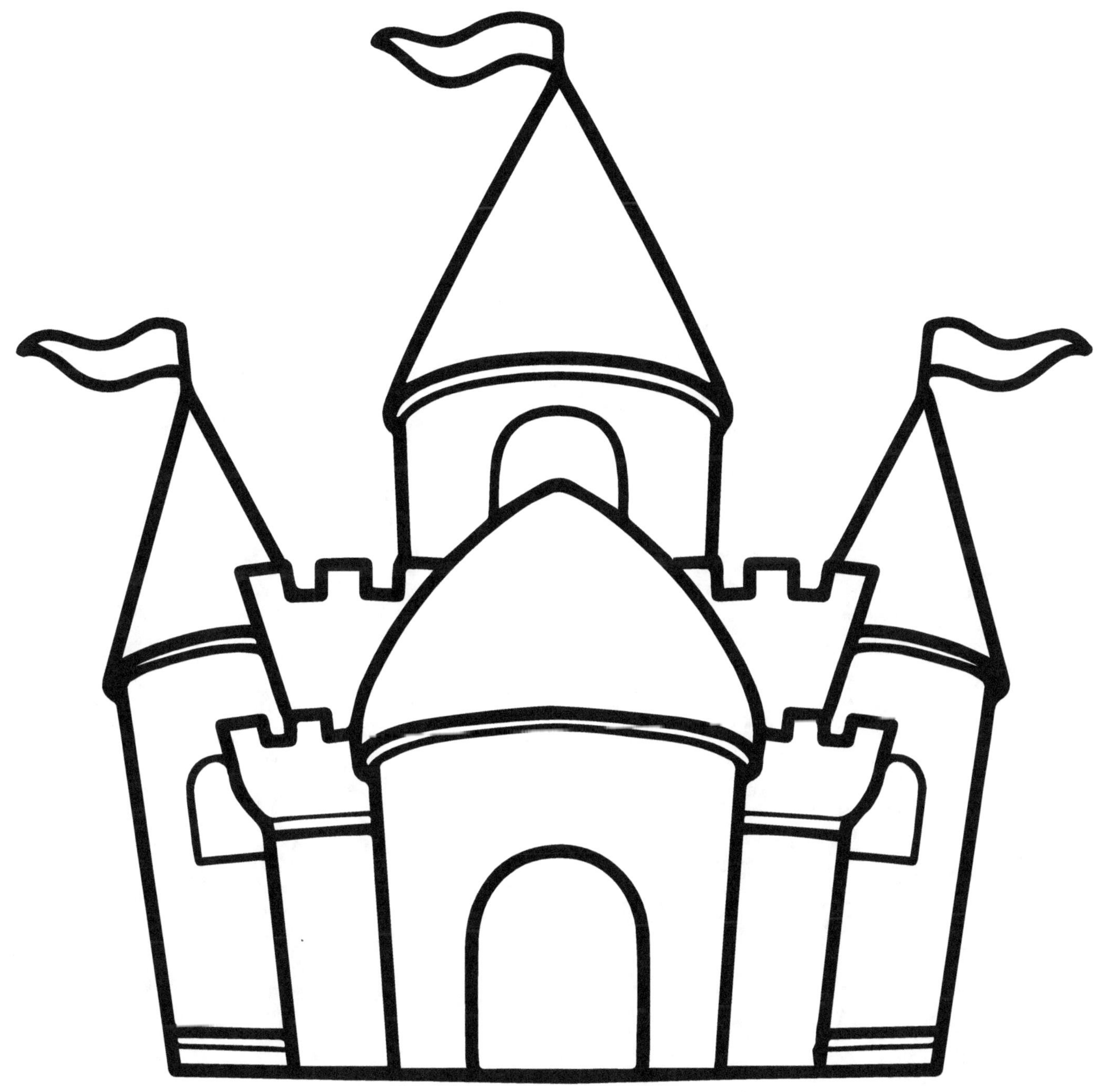

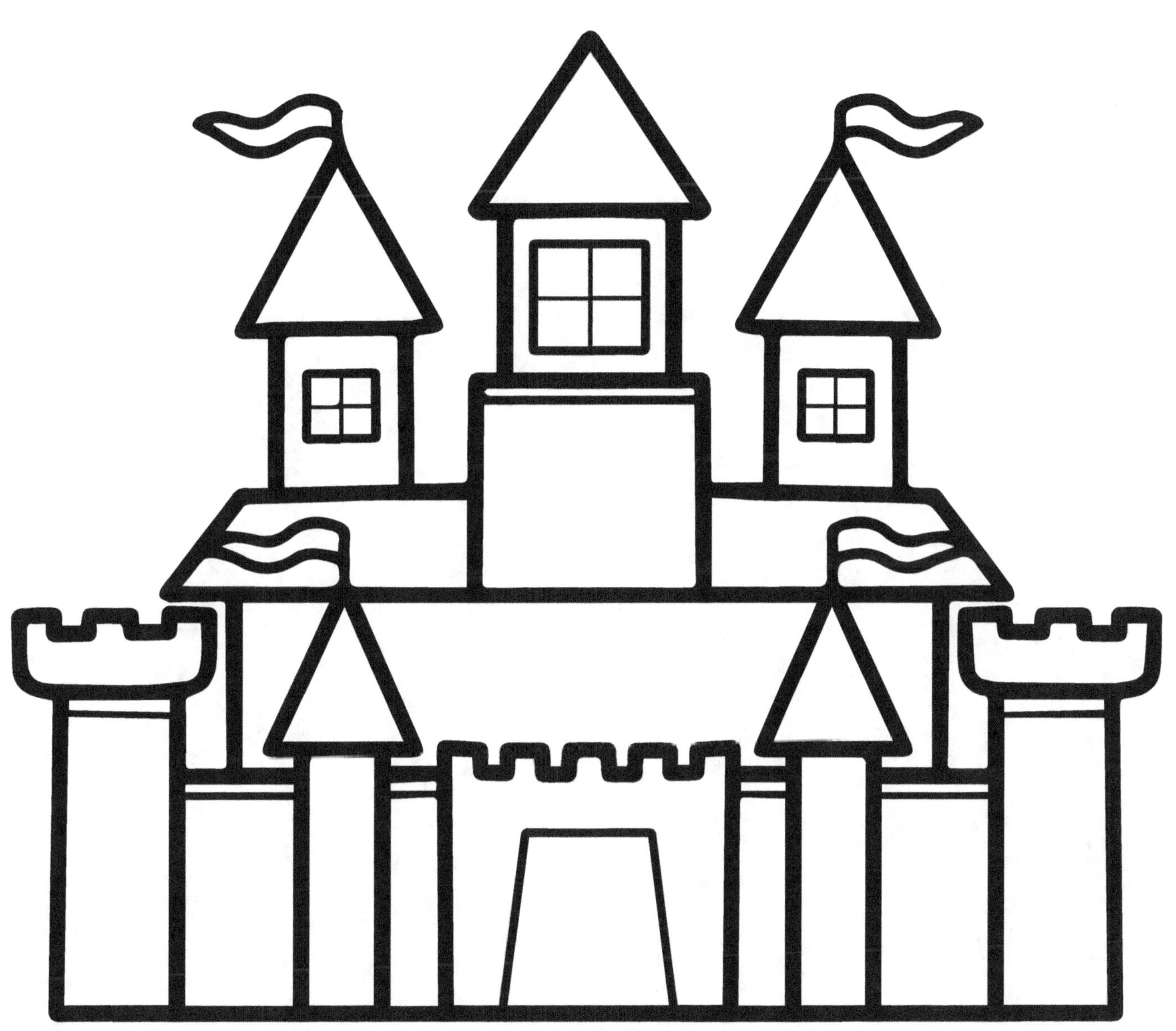

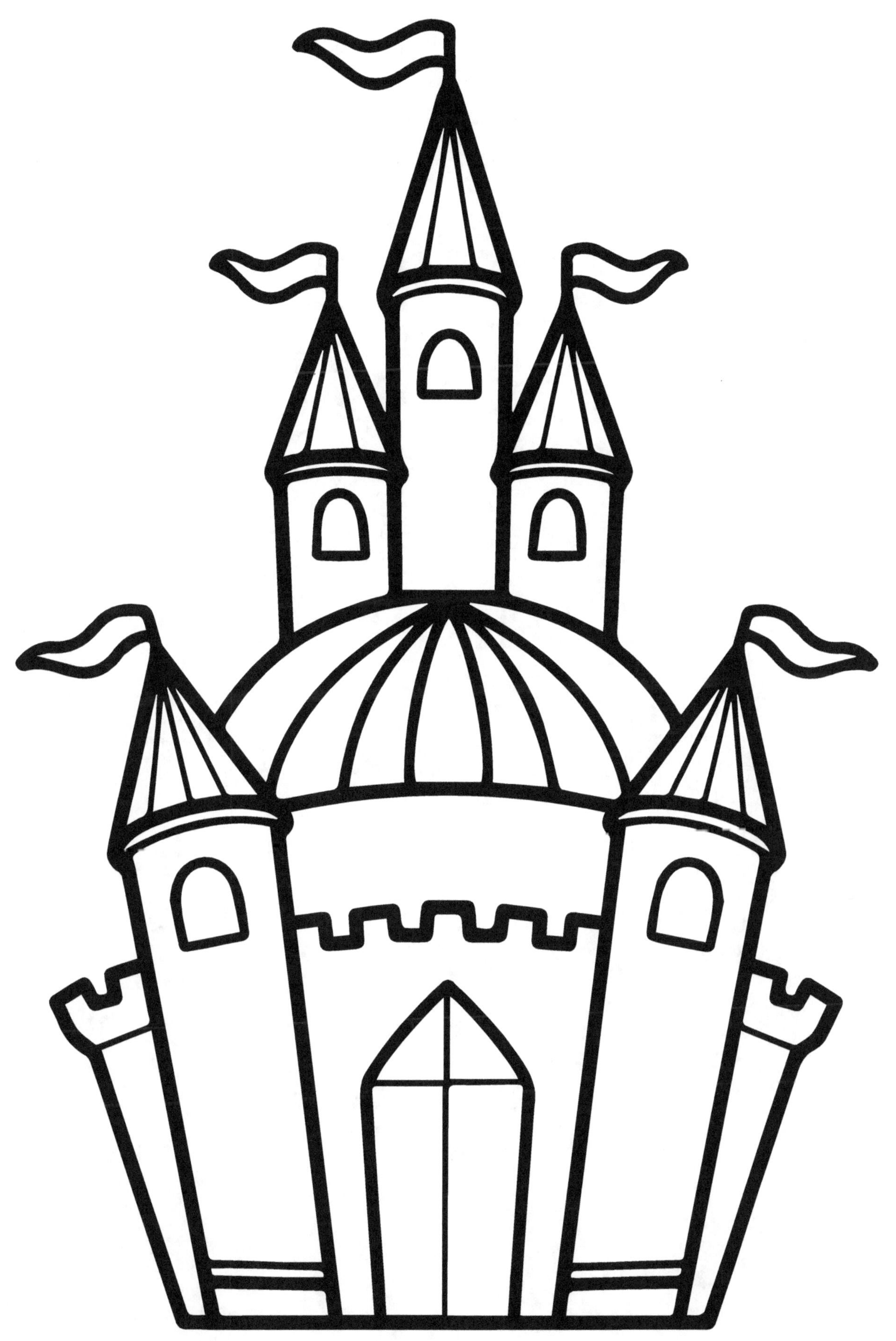

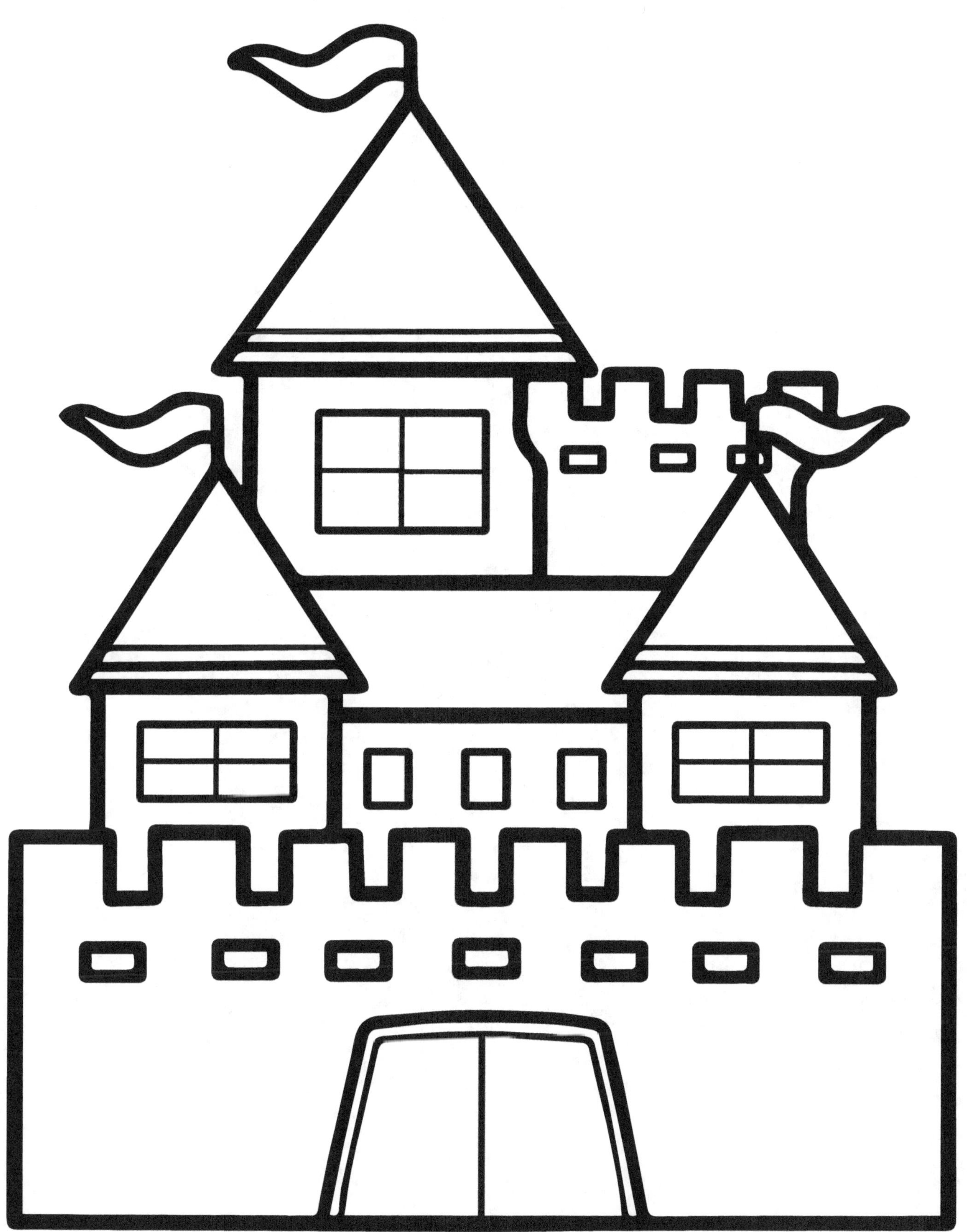

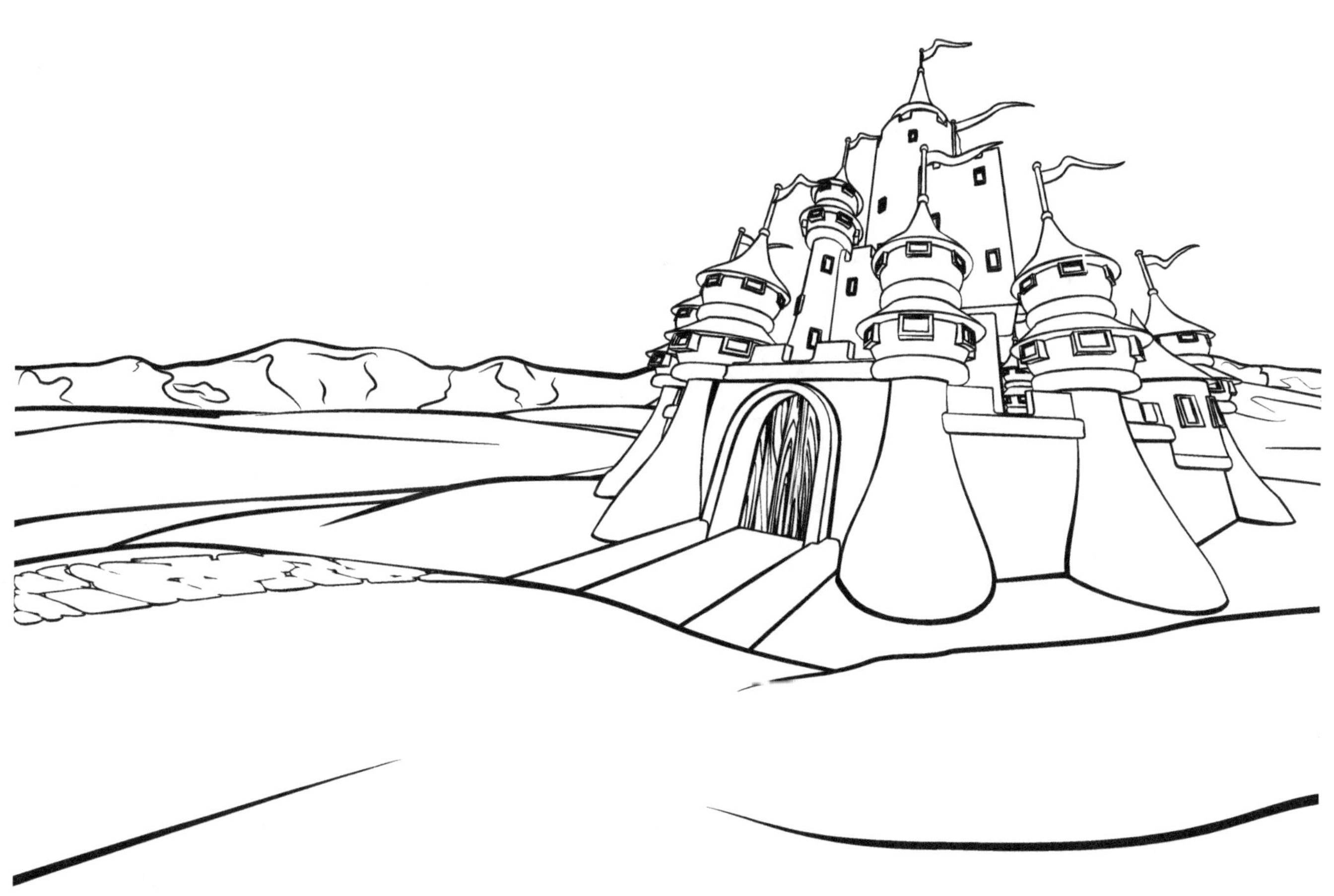

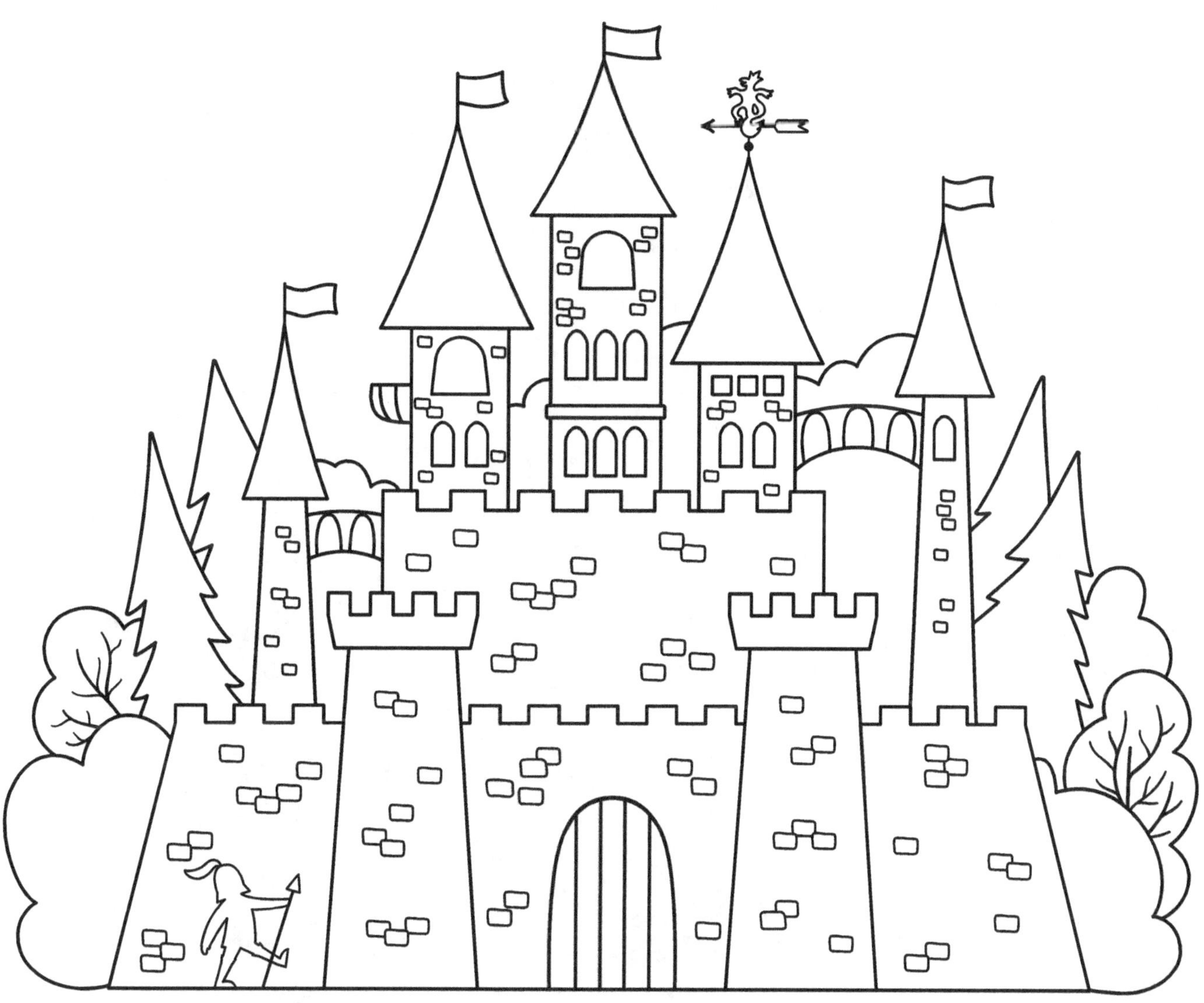

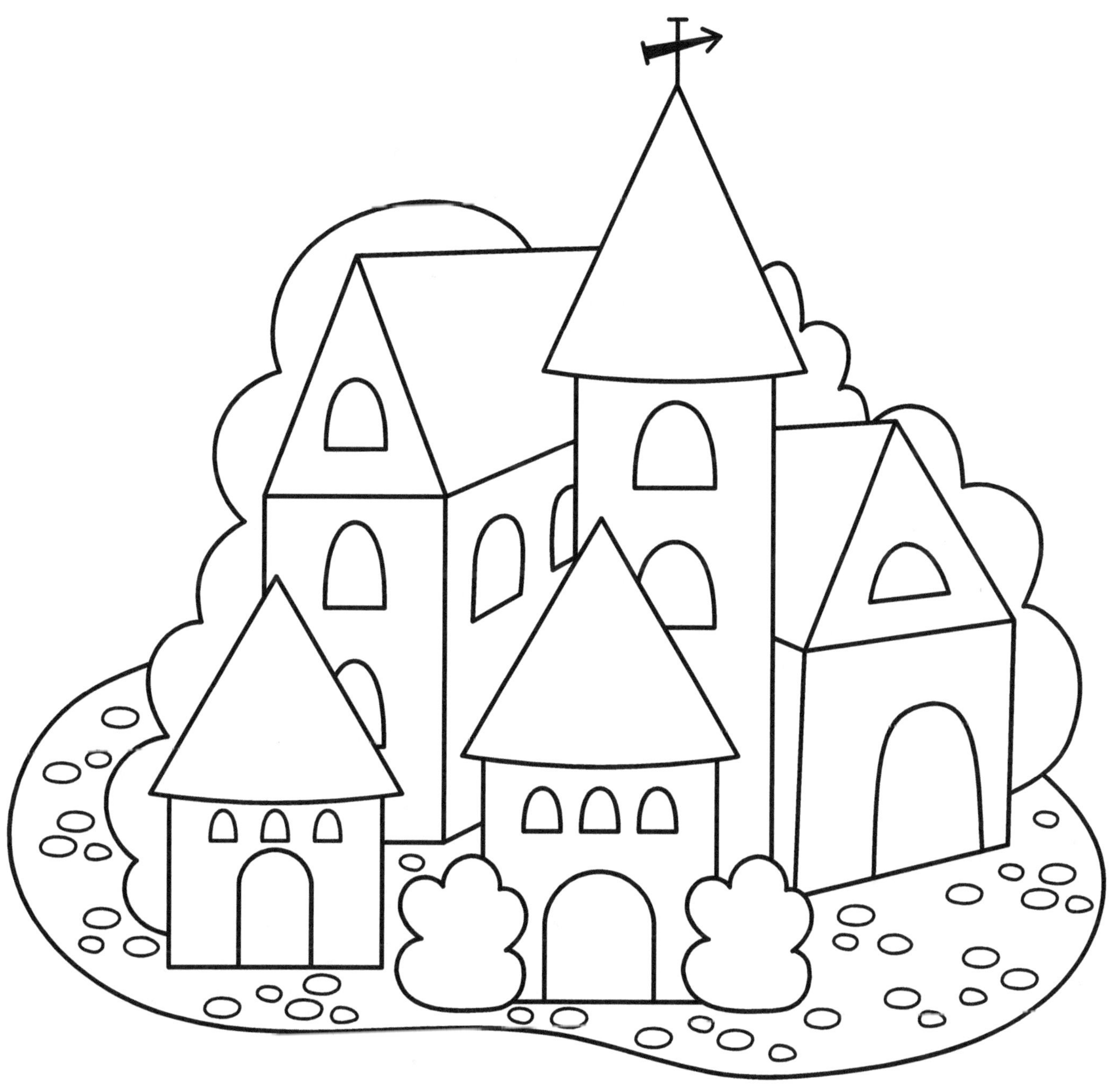

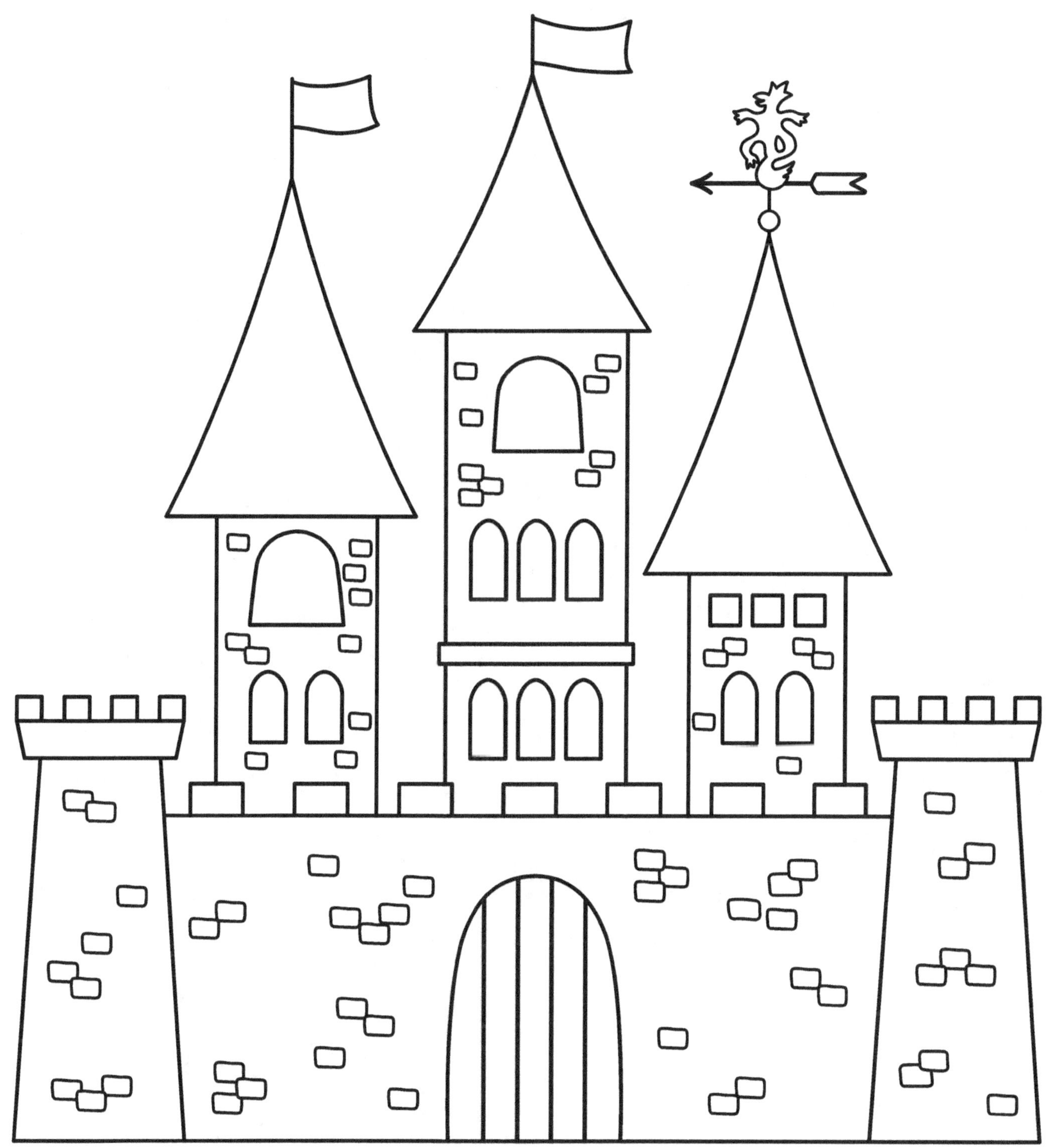

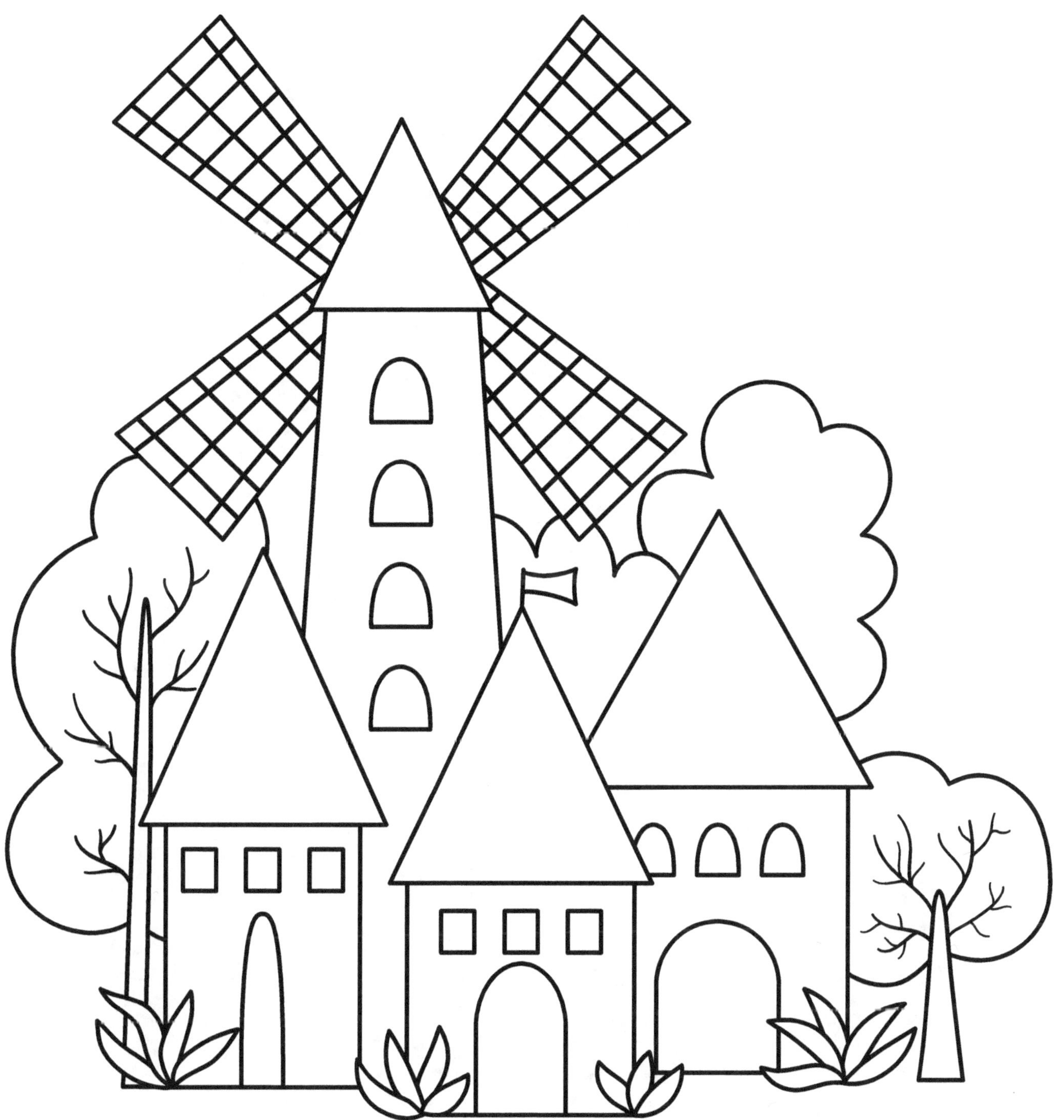

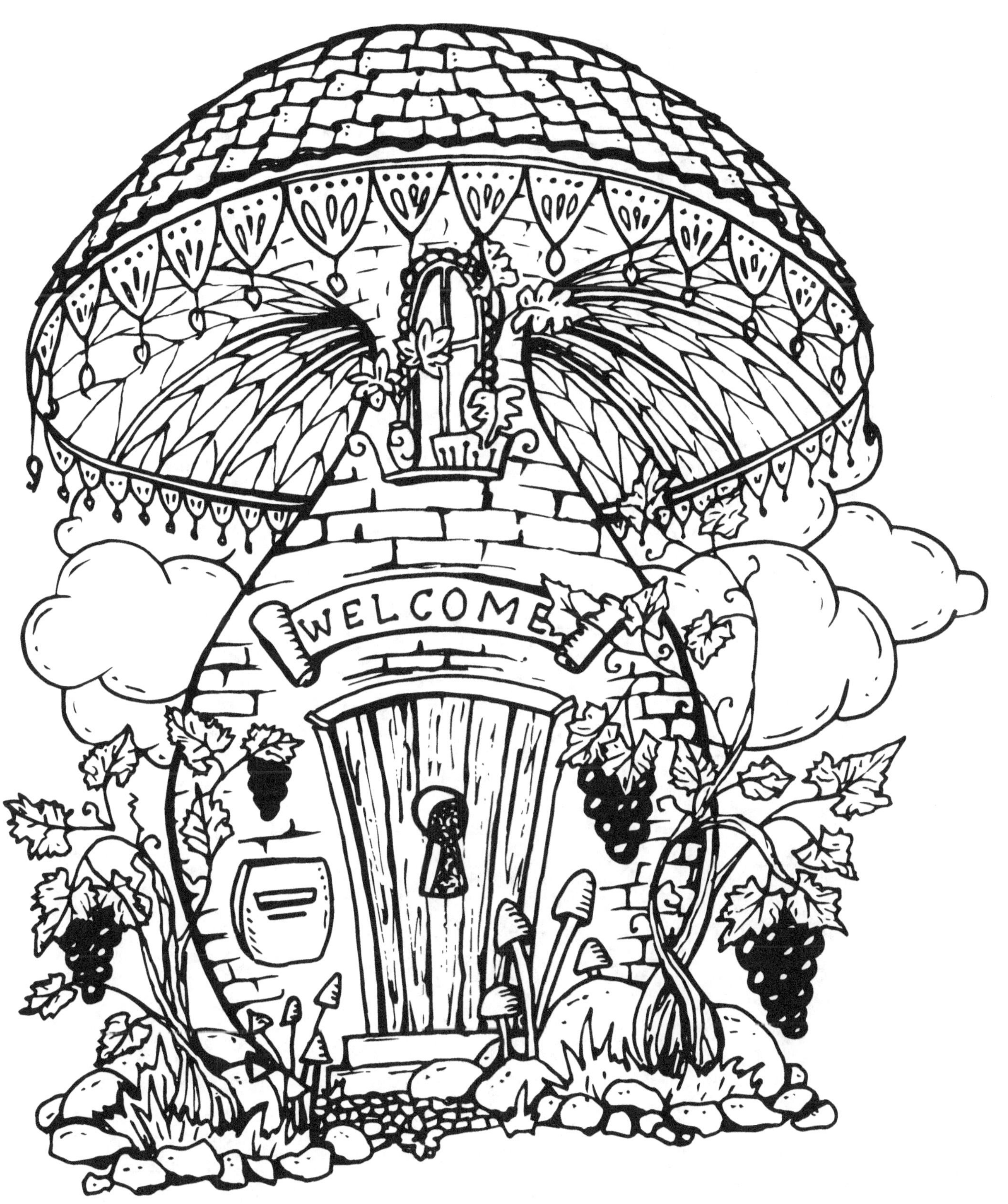
WELCOME

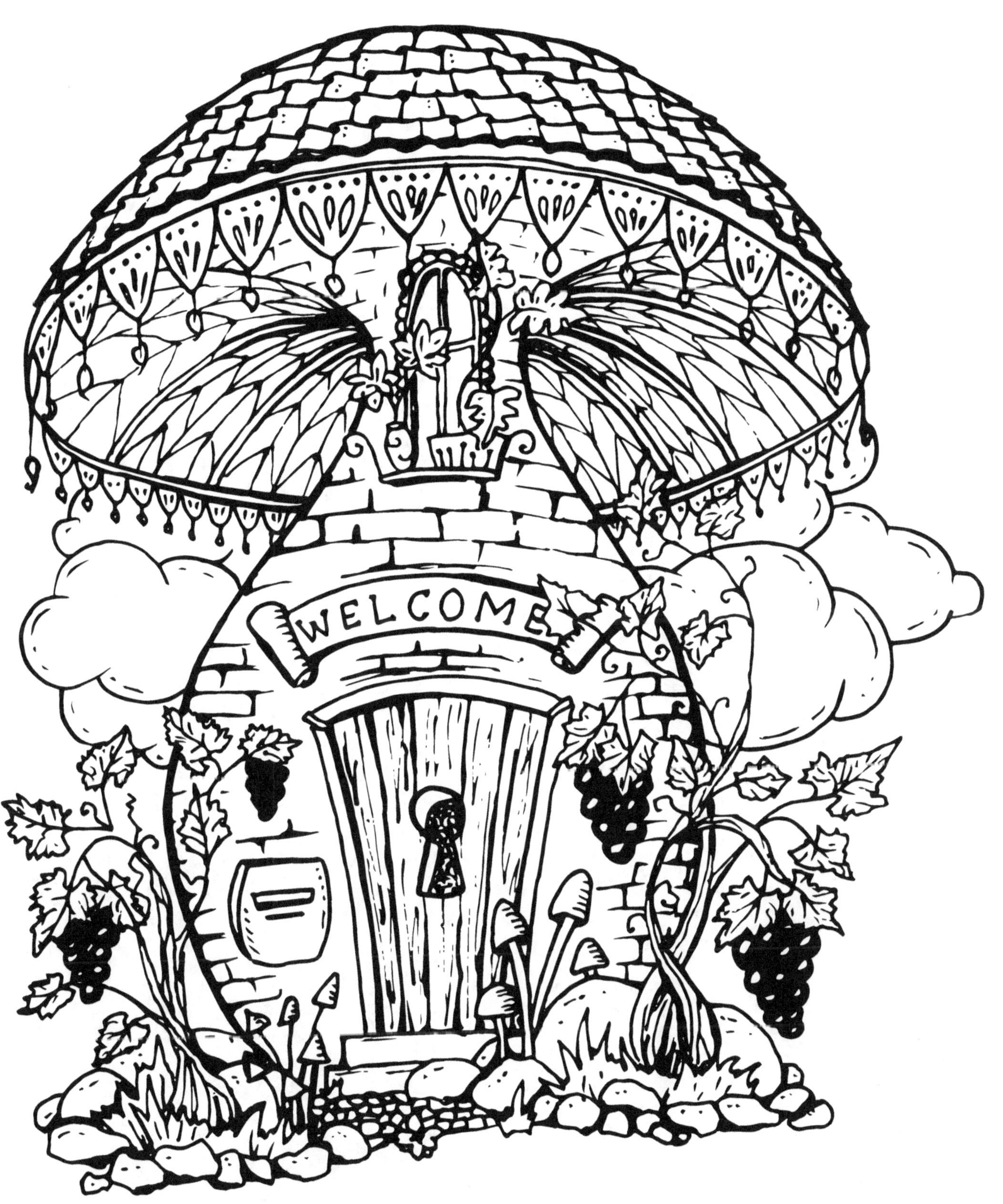
WELCOME

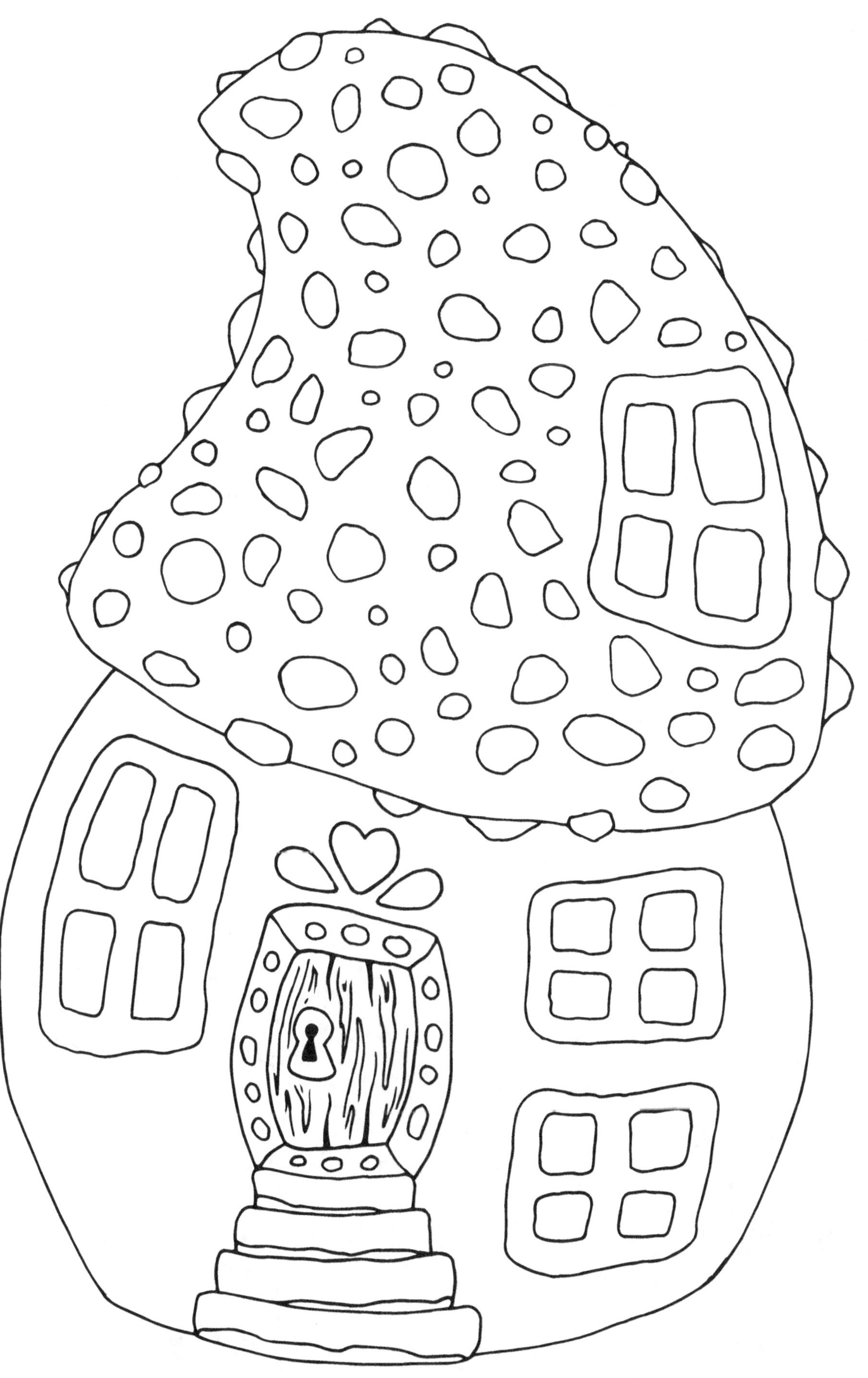

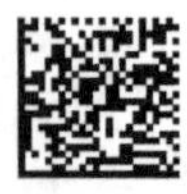